Big Business

Economic Power in a Free Society

Big
Business
Economic Power in a Free Society

Advisory Editor
LEON STEIN

Editorial Board
Stuart Bruchey
Thomas C. Cochran

A NOTE ABOUT THIS BOOK

The author discusses the inconstancy of the concept of economic virtue with
special reference to the western frontier farmer and businessman and, by contrast,
the self-made millionaire in oil, iron, and steel. The emphasis is on religious roots,
Puritan ethics and good works through great fortunes. The relativity of business
success is measured against changing interpretations of thrift, caution, prudence,
foresight, industry and honesty. "As business conditions changed and as business-
men's ideas of money making under new conditions changed," the author notes,
"new virtues began to be stressed."

ECONOMIC VIRTUES IN THE UNITED STATES

A History and an Interpretation

By
DONALD McCONNELL

ARNO PRESS
A New York Times Company
New York / 1973

Reprint Edition 1973 by Arno Press Inc.

Reprinted from a copy in
. The University of Illinois Library

BIG BUSINESS: Economic Power in a Free Society
ISBN for complete set: 0-405-05070-4
See last pages of this volume for titles.

Manufactured in the United States of America

———◆———

Library of Congress Cataloging in Publication Data

McConnell, Donald William, 1901–
  Economic virtues in the United States.

  (Big business: economic power in a free society)
  Originally presented as the author's thesis, Columbia
University.
  Bibliography: p.
  1. United States—Economic conditions. 2. National
characteristics. American. 3. Business ethics.
I. Title. II. Series.
HC103.M3 1973   330.9'73   73-2520
ISBN 0-405-05100-X

ECONOMIC VIRTUES IN THE UNITED STATES

A History and an Interpretation

By
DONALD McCONNELL

Submitted in partial fulfillment
of the requirements for the
degree of Doctor of Philosophy,
in the Faculty of Political
Science, Columbia University.

NEW YORK
1930

Printed in the United States of America

TABLE OF CONTENTS

PREFACE

PARSIMONY, thrift, prudence, foresight, industry, and honesty, when practiced by individuals, are the traditional economic virtues in western civilization. It is thought that capital is increased by parsimony and thrift; the capital is then used in various industries and this leads to the employment of greater numbers of workers and to the production of more commodities for society as a whole. This is thought not merely beneficial for society but absolutely necessary if a country is to evade ruin. Adam Smith asserted that, "If the prodigality of some was not compensated by the frugality of others, the conduct of every prodigal, by feeding the idle with the bread of the industrious, tends not only to beggar himself, but to impoverish the country."[1]

The individual is not thinking of the welfare of society while he is being thrifty or industrious. It is his own welfare that concerns him. But in the protection of his own interest, the welfare of society is automatically protected and increased. Thus any difficulties in which particular classes find themselves are easily solved by an increased effort at prudence, thrift, industry, etc. Ricardo, in discussing the conditions of the working class in England, said, "By gradually contracting the sphere of the poor laws, by impressing on the poor the value of independence, by teaching them that they must look not to systematic or casual charity, but to their own exertions for support, that prudence and forethought are neither unnecessary nor unprofitable virtues, we shall by degrees approach a sounder and more healthful state."[2] Here an appeal to the virtues is not merely an explanation of economic activity; it is a policy for the solution of economic problems. In short, these economists considered any behavior which they thought would lead to what they considered to be the "economic welfare" of society as economic virtues.

These traditional virtues have been highly regarded in America. In fact, one of the distinctions made between the United States and Europe is the greater prevalence of "self-help"

7

and individualism in the former than in the latter. It is the purpose of this study to investigate the process by which the traditional virtues have become so widely accepted in the United States, to attempt to discover what is meant by the statement that the virtues lead to the "economic welfare" of society, to see how the virtues have been used to solve various economic problems, and to see if the traditional virtues are being displaced by other "economic virtues."

Instead of attempting to cover the whole of economic history in the United States emphasis will be placed on certain phases of American economic development. The pioneer hunters and farmers on the frontier, the business groups in the frontier regions, and some of the later industrialists, more particularly those in the oil and steel industries, will be studied. Then the development of the economic virtues and the uses to which they have been put during the twentieth century will be briefly considered.

Obviously, this ignores wide areas of American economic life such as the Colonial merchants and large landholders, the planters of the South before the Civil War, the gold and silver miners in the far West, organized labor groups, to mention only a few of those groups that are not considered. However, the samples studied may throw some light on economic virtues in the United States and the rôle these virtues play in economic activity.

In the preparation of this dissertation the author is indebted to Professor J. M. Clark for many valuable suggestions and criticisms.

FOOTNOTES FOR PREFACE

[1] Adam Smith, *The Wealth of Nations*, Everyman's Edition. Vol. I, p. 303.
[2] Ricardo, *The Principles of Political Economy and Taxation*, Everyman's Edition, p. 62.

CHAPTER I

THE INFLUENCE OF THE FRONTIER ON ECONOMIC VIRTUES

THE frontier has attracted the attention of scholars because of its presumed influence on the later developments of society.[1] This interest in frontier life and its influence is particularly strong in the United States. And for a very good reason. The American frontier did not disappear until about 1890. Frontier life continuously asserted its influence during the "formative period" of American development. Furthermore, the habits of thought and action engendered on the frontier are thought to be with us yet, since the frontier disappeared so recently.[2]

The frontier has been described as a rather indefinite area fading into the wilderness on the one side and merging into civilization on the other, an area in which the first rude efforts to eke out a living and subjugate the natural environment to the needs of man are attempted. Historians have discovered many of the so-called American traits of character in frontier life. One sees the frontier as the cradle of independence, equality, and democracy.[3] Another observes that the frontiersmen had an intense fondness for the woods and a lonely restless life. Consequently, "they pushed independence to an extreme; they did not wish to work for others or to rent land from others."[4] Another historian discovered that the essential qualities for success on the frontier were "initiative, resourcefulness, quick, confident, and sure judgment."[5] These various traits of behavior have been sometimes considered peculiarly American. Where have individual enterprise and "self-help" been more glorified? Before concluding that such traits came from the frontier it may be well to inquire into the nature of frontier life more closely.

One difficulty in getting an accurate description of frontier life is that the frontier has not escaped the attention of those anxious to romanticize early American life.[6] W. C. Macleod says

9

that many early documents have been destroyed lest the frontiersmen be portrayed in an ignominious light.[7] There is the picture of Daniel Boone, trail maker and explorer of the wilderness, who relies on his own skill and ingenuity for protection from the Indians; who, by his knowledge of the forest and his observance of the ways of animals, can provide himself with food and shelter. He likes the lonely life of the forest. As settlement follows his trail and crowds about him, he sets out again and disappears into the woods where he may be his own master. Later researches force a revision of this description. It is true that he was a hunter and a scout. However, when he made his famous trip into Kentucky in 1769 he was not opening a new trail for civilization. The Wilderness Trail had been known for some time. He was not escaping the presence of settlers who pressed about him. His trip was a business proposition. Richard Henderson of the Transylvania Company had hired him to mark off some land suitable for sale to prospective purchasers in the east. And Boone looked wistfully toward a settled existence in the more populous lands to the east. His employment was not sufficiently remunerative to fulfill his hopes.[8]

The historians have drawn some of their conclusions concerning the enterprise of the frontiersmen from such descriptions as the following:

It was they (the first inhabitants) who began to clear these fertile countries, and wrested them from the savages who ferociously disputed their right; it was they, in short, who made themselves masters of the possessions, after five or six years' bloody war; but the long habit of a wandering and idle life has prevented their enjoying the fruits of their labors, and profiting by the very price to which these lands have risen in so short a time. They have emigrated to more remote parts of the country, and formed new settlements. It will be the same with most of those who inhabit the borders of Ohio. The same inclination that led them there will induce them to emigrate from it. To the latter will succeed fresh emigrants, coming also from the Atlantic states, who will desert their possessions to go in quest of a milder climate and a more fertile soil. . . . The last comers . . . will clear a greater quantity of the land, and be as industrious and persevering in the melioration of their new possessions as the former were indolent in everything, being so fond of hunting.[9]

Another observer of early western life says:

Generally, in all the western settlements, three classes, like the waves of the ocean, have rolled one after the other. First comes the pioneer, who depends for the subsistence of his family chiefly upon the natural growth of vegetation, called the "range," and the proceeds of hunting. His implements of agriculture are rude, chiefly of his own make, and his efforts directed mainly to a crop of corn and a "truck patch." The last is a rude garden for growing cabbage, beans, corn for roasting ears, cucumbers, and potatoes. A log cabin, and, occasionally, a stable and corn-crib, and a field of a dozen acres, the timber girdled or "deadened," and fenced, are enough for his occupancy. It is quite immaterial whether he ever becomes the owner of the soil. He is the occupant for the time being, pays no rent, and feels as independent as the "lord of the manor." With a horse, cow, and one or two breeders of swine, he strikes into the woods with his family, and becomes the founder of a new county, or perhaps state. He builds his cabin, gathers around him a few other families of similar tastes and habits, and occupies till the range is somewhat subdued, and hunting a little precarious, or, which is more frequently the case, till the neighbors crowd around, roads, bridges, and fields annoy him, and he lacks elbow room. The preemption law enables him to dispose of his cabin and cornfield to the next class of emigrants; and, to employ his own figures, he "breaks for the high timber," "clears out for the New Purchase," or migrates to Arkansas or Texas, to work the same process over.

The next class of emigrants purchase the lands, add field to field, clear out the roads, throw rough bridges over streams, put up hewn log houses with glass windows and brick or stone chimneys, occasionally plant orchards, build mills, schoolhouses, court-houses, etc., and exhibit the picture and forms of plain, frugal, civilized life.

Another wave rolls on. The men of capital and enterprise come. The settler is ready to sell out and take the advantage of the rise in property, push farther into the interior and become, himself, a man of capital and enterprise in turn. The small village rises to a spacious town or city; substantial edifices of brick, extensive fields, orchards, gardens, colleges, and churches are seen. Broadcloths, silks, leghorns, crapes, and all the refinements, luxuries, elegancies, frivolities, and fashions are in vogue.

Thus wave after wave is rolling westward; the real Eldorado is still farther on.

A portion of the two first classes remain stationary amidst the general movement, improve their habits and condition, and rise in the scale of society.[10]

Perhaps it is possible to conclude from these descriptions that the frontiersmen were enterprising and independent people. However, a bit more should be known about the frontiersmen before any conclusion is reached. An important aspect of the descriptions is that they discriminate between classes.[11] There are the hunters, the farmers, and the men of business and enterprise. The distinction between the two first classes is not particularly important since hunters devote part of their time to farming and farmers spend some time hunting. The difference is a matter of degree.[12] Between the hunter-farmer group on the one side and the business group on the other there is sufficient difference to justify a separate study of the respective groups.

Another thing about the descriptions. The different classes appear in a chronological sequence that is not historically accurate. In many parts of the West the business men, particularly speculators, appeared before the hunters and farmers. From an early time the Easterners were interested in the West as a profitable speculation. Such men as George Washington, Benjamin Franklin, and Patrick Henry hoped to acquire easy fortune from the expected rise in western land values.[13] Speculators prospected for land that appeared favorable for settlement, then divided the chosen area into town lots and sold the lots to Easterners. Louisville, Kentucky, was founded in this manner. The following is an advertisement of lots in the town:

The Subscribers, Patentees of Land at the Falls of the Ohio, hereby inform the Publick that they intend to lay out a Town there in the Most convenient Place. The Lots to be 80 Feet front and 240 deep. The number of Lots that shall be laid off at first will depend on the Number of Applications. The Purchase Money of each Lot to be four Spanish Dollars, and one Dollar per Annum Quitrent for ever. . . . The advantageous Situation of that Place, formed by Nature as a temporary Magazine, or Repository, to receive the produce of the very extensive and fertile

Country on the Ohio and its Branches as well as the necessary
Merchandises suitable for the Inhabitants that shall emigrate into
the country (as Boats of fifty Tuns Burthen may be navigated
from New Orleans up to the Town) is sufficient to recommend
it; but when it is considered how liberal, nay profuse, Nature has
been to it otherwise, in stocking it so abundantly that the slightest
Industry may supply the most numerous Family with the greatest
Plenty and amazing Variety of Fish, Fowl, and Flesh; the Fer-
tility of the Soil, and Facility of Cultivation, that fit it for producing Commodities of great Value with little Labour; the Whole-
someness of the Waters, and Serenity of the Air, which render
it healthy; and when Property may be so easily acquired, we may,
with Certainty, affirm that it will in a short Time be equalled by
a few inland Places on the American Continent.

JOHN CAMPBELL—JOHN CONNOLLY.[14]

Apparently the lonely and isolated hunter and farmer was
not always a necessary precursor to settlements. In Wisconsin
and Minnesota the lumber industry followed fur-trading. And
the farmers as a distinct group did not appear until after the
lumber industry was well developed.[15] Regardless of the vagaries
of chronology, the pioneer hunter-farmers and the men of business represented distinct groups. Their economic behavior was
different, as were their conceptions of economic virtues.

In order to narrow the study somewhat the hunter-farmer
frontier will be considered in the area that is at present included
within the boundaries of Pennsylvania, Kentucky, Ohio, Indiana,
Illinois, Missouri, Michigan, and Wisconsin. In point of time
the first half of the nineteenth century will be emphasized.

The occupations of the frontiersmen cannot be explained by
the motives which led them to the West. The motives were too
numerous. Many of them started with the hope of making their
fortunes in the West; some small farmers were attempting to
escape the competition of slave labor in the South; some from New
England moved west with the firm conviction that no soil could
be more barren than the stony fields they had left; scoundrels, the
socially ostracized, and fugitives from justice sought freedom in
the West; not a few hoped to build the new Utopia in the western
country. After their arrival in the West, particularly after cross-

ing the Allegheny mountains, their contact with the East was difficult and infrequent. The pioneers, at least for a time, developed a life distinctly different from that left behind. Many of the more obvious differences between the types that went to the frontier disappeared. Under the new conditions life became highly standardized.

One of the characteristics of this new life was continual movement from one place to another. Did this continual change of habitat mean an enterprising spirit, a behavior trait that has since been influential in American economic life? If not, how else is it to be explained?

The individual interested in hunting was almost forced to move about because the game was plentiful only in sparsely settled areas. Frequently he was a nomad, packing up his few belongings and taking his family with him as he followed the game. Doddridge described this process as he observed it in Western Pennsylvania and Western Virginia. He said:

Many of the backwoodsmen forsook civilization, even after they had built comfortable homes for themselves. They no longer had the chance of a "fall hunt"! . . . They wanted elbow room. They therefore sold out and fled to the forest of the frontier settlements, choosing rather to encounter the toil of turning the wilderness into fruitful fields a second time, and even risk an Indian war, rather than endure the inconvenience of a crowded settlement.[16]

A crowded settlement scattered the game and hunting became difficult if not impossible. In order to survive, the hunters had to change their habits of life and maintain a settled existence. But this was too great an effort for most of them. It was much easier to move to a new area where they could continue their old ways than to remain where they were and adopt the new life that a crowded settlement and a settled existence would force upon them.

Among those who devoted most of their time to farming the same mobility was noticed.[17] The description by Sir Charles Lyell of one of these farmer movers, whom he met on a steamboat going from Mobile to New Orleans, was typical of many of the farmers. "He was, I found, one of those resolute pioneers of the wilderness, who, after building a log house, clearing the forest, and improving some hundred acres of wild ground by years of labor, sells the farm, and migrates again to another part of the uncleared forest, repeating this operation three or four times in the course of his life."[18] This type of moving revealed a certain fear and dread of change rather than a desire for it. One frontier was very much like the last. In each new area the farmer could follow his customary mode of life without having to worry about learning new ways of doing things and adjusting himself to the new situation created by the larger population about him. Nor was it always obvious that he was attempting to improve his economic position by such movement. The easiest way for a pioneer farmer to increase his fortune was to "sit tight" until the larger settlement of people about him created a greater demand for the land, and then to sell out. But relatively few did this. And even in successive removals from one place to another the new location was not improved greatly over the preceding.[19]

The early pioneers did not impress observers with their enterprising spirit. They fled at the news of new arrivals. One observer further commented on them, "The hunters are as persevering as savages, and as indolent. They cultivate indolence as a privilege: 'You English are very industrious, but we have freedom.' And thus they exist in yawning indifference, surrounded with nuisances and petty wants, the first to be removed, and the latter supplied by a tenth of the time loitered away in their innumerable idle days."[20]

Some of the Indian tribes observed that the early pioneers lacked enterprise and seemed to be on the frontier because they could not get along elsewhere. In 1812 the government proposed to buy from the Indians some land northwest of the Ohio. The Indians suggested that the money be paid to the settlers since the settlers were so poor and apparently could not survive elsewhere.[21]

The romanticized Davy Crockett is a fair example of the type of enterprise encountered on the frontier. "In the course of successive removals he traversed the entire length of Tennessee, drinking, hunting, talking, speculating, begetting children, scratching a few acres of land 'to make his crap,' yet living for the most part off the country; and his last squatting place on the Obion river, seven miles from the nearest neighbor, was as primitive as the first. . . . He was never much given to mending fences or enlarging his plowland."[22]

These descriptions hardly portray the enterprising individual anxious to get ahead in the world. The restlessness of the frontiersmen was due to inertia, not enterprise. The type of life to which they were habituated was more easily followed in relative isolation. A crowded settlement brought a type of life that was strange. If they were to accept the new life a change of habits was necessary—an act not willingly contemplated or easily attained. The alternative was to move. This was more to the pioneers' liking.

Other traits have been supposed to characterize the pioneer hunter-farmer's existence. For example, "self-help" and individualism. Again, this must be interpreted in terms of the pioneer's own life, not in terms of later developments. Individualism, as it is commonly understood, assumes an elaborate system of exchanges. There would be little point in one's specializing in a certain line if there were not other specialists with whom one's goods could be exchanged. There was little specialization on the frontier. Consequently it was difficult for an "unseen hand" to guide individuals to an end "that was no part of their original intention," that is, to the welfare of society. The pioneers could not rely on free private enterprise as a means of building homes or gathering crops. These activities demanded co-operative activity. The pioneers emphasized the collective activities and then let individual activity take care of itself after the collective activities were attended to.

The members of the frontier communities were dependent upon one another in much of their social and economic life. In parts of the Old Southwest where the pioneers got little help from the government for protection from the Indians, they had to provide for the collective defense of their settlement. Doddridge says:

The whole populations of the frontiers huddled together in their little forts, left the country with every appearance of a deserted region. . . . Every man was a soldier and from early in the spring until late in the fall was almost continually in arms. Their work was often carried out by parties, each one of whom had his rifle and everything else belonging to his wardrobe. These were deposited in some central place in the field. A sentinel was stationed on the outside of the fence, so that on the least alarm the whole company repaired to their arms and were ready for the combat in a moment.[23]

If one became too enterprising in the cultivation of the fields and worked alone one might be killed in a sudden attack by the Indians. During the seventeenth century, when the frontier line was farther east, Indian wars were disastrous when the settlement was too thinly diffused. A report by the colonists on one of these wars gave as one of its causes the fact that "the colonists, . . . with a view each to push forward his own advantage, separated themselves from one another and settled far in the interior, the better to drive trade with the Indians. . . ." The result was that the isolated individuals could not protect themselves.[24] Individual enterprise, in areas where the whites had provoked the Indians to warfare, was rather severely punished.

Besides this collective defense there was collective and co-operative economic activity which persisted in many frontier settlements long after collective defense had disappeared. The amount of collective work varied with different settlements, but in some places it seemed almost communistic. For example, a number of immigrants to Missouri arrived from Kentucky and Indiana in 1817.

They built their cabins along the trail, just far enough apart to enable the women to raise chickens. The settlers were in a certain sense communists, particularly on the borders of Howard and Saline Counties. Their work was largely on the cooperative plan. They cleared and fenced a large field, which they divided into lots without any partition fences. There every man planted his crop in the "Big Field," as it was called. The field increased from forty to one thousand acres. Each settler was entitled to cultivate what he cleared and helped to fence; that is, made rails for.[25]

Self-help was recognized since the individual cultivated the land he had cleared. But the group worked together and to some extent the individual enterprise was regulated by the activity of the whole group.

Some of the French communities transplanted European agricultural organization to the new area. The open field system and the village community were set up in the West. A Big Field was cultivated and although the holdings were individual the cattle were turned into the commons at a fixed date. The people did not live on their individual holdings, but dwelt together in the village community.[26]

In other parts of the West there was much collective activity even though the settlers did not cooperatively clear and till a "Big Field." In Ohio most of the farmers owned the land they lived upon and all worked with their own hands, whether they hired help or not.[27] But this did not mean that each individual relied on his own efforts for his subsistence. Houses and barns were erected with the assistance of neighbors. "Particularly remarkable was the general equality and the general dependence of all upon the neighborly kindness and good offices of others," says Howells. "Their houses and barns were built of logs, and were raised by the collection of many neighbors together on one day, whose united strength was necessary to the handling of the logs. As every man was ready with the axe and understood this work, all came together within the circle where the raising was to be done, and all worked together with about equal skill. . . . It was the custom always to send one from a family to help so that you could claim like assistance in return."[28]

Threshing and harvesting were frequently collective enterprises. The implements were often primitive. Where the flail was used for threshing a farmer relied on his neighbors for assistance. Here again "team-work" was necessary for the task to be done properly. Considerable skill was necessary to wield the flail and keep in stroke with the others. "He who failed to keep the stroke properly would often suffer for his carelessness by a blow from one of the conflicting and rebounding flails."[29] Corn-husking was another collective enterprise. It was the excuse for a social gathering and was often performed in the spirit of a game or contest. The unhusked corn was placed in a long row. Then two leaders chose sides and at a given signal the two groups started at the ends of the row and worked toward the center. The side that husked its corn and arrived at the center first was the winner. The reward usually was liberal quantities of whiskey. These huskings survived as social events long after they ceased to be matters of economic necessity. Log-rolling, flax pullings, apple paring bees, quiltings and wood choppings were some of the other activities that assumed a collective aspect.

Such "self-help" as existed on the frontier fitted into this framework of cooperative activity. And the "self-help" developed out of a lack of specialization. The frontier communities had little access to the manufactured goods of the East, and had to rely on their own efforts for most of the things they used.

A very few merchants supplied them with the few necessaries which could not be produced or manufactured at home. The farmer raised his own provisions; tea and coffee were scarcely used, except on some grand occasions. The farmer's sheep furnished wool for his winter clothing; he raised cotton and flax for his summer clothing. His wife and daughters spun, wove, and made it into garments. A little copperas and indigo, with the bark of trees, furnished dye stuffs for coloring. . . . Each farmer as a general thing built his own house, made his own plows and harness, bedsteads, chairs, stools, cupboards, and tables.[30]

One of the pioneers illustrates the diversity of things done within the household by enumerating the tasks in which he assisted when a boy. He helped with broom making, soap making, cheese making, churning, hog killing, sausage making, dyeing, sheep washing and shearing, wool carding, and spinning.[31] So great was the amount of this household manufacture in the early years of the nineteenth century that it seemed the pioneers were deliberately attempting to maintain independence from the outside world.[32]

Few individuals confined their entire attention to these manufactures. It has been estimated that ninety-nine out of every hundred in Illinois in 1818 were farmers.[33] Along with this farming they had to attend to their household manufactures. And these different tasks were performed with relatively few tools. In this situation a number of jacks-of-all-trades developed who could put their hands to a number of jobs without doing any of them remarkably well. Great ingenuity was developed in adapting a few tools to a variety of uses. James Hall says:

> The dexterity of the backwoodsman in the use of the axe is also remarkable; yet it ceases to be so regarded, when we reflect on the variety of uses to which this implement is applied, and that it in fact enters into almost all the occupations of the pioneer. In clearing lands, building houses, making fences, providing fuel, the axe is used; in tilling his fields, the farmer is continually interrupted to cut away the trees that have fallen in his enclosures and the roots that impede his plow; the path of the surveyor is cleared by the axe, and his lines and corners marked by this implement; roads are opened and bridges made with the axe; the first court-houses and jails are fashioned of logs, with the same tool; in labor or hunting, in traveling by land or water, the axe is ever the companion of the backwoodsman.[34]

The jack-of-all-trades was admired for his cleverness and ingenuity rather than for the thoroughness with which he did his work. The story is told of a farmer who was plowing his field. His horse's harness and the plow he was using were made with his own hands. When he stopped for dinner his son thought he could put an end to plowing for the day by hiding one of the hames. His father would have to stop and construct another one. Much to his surprise his father took off the leather trousers he was wearing, stuffed them with stubble, put them in place of the wooden hames and went on about his plowing as barelegged as the day he was born.[35] The farmers referred to this type of resourcefulness as inventiveness.

One was admired for putting one tool to a variety of uses. Thoroughness with which work was done was not carefully examined if one were clever and ingenious in devising ways of getting the work accomplished at all. The jack-of-all-trades was a man of some standing. The inventiveness was made necessary by a scarcity of labor in the West and a lack of manufactured implements.[36] The Americans gloried in their inventiveness and erected it into a national virtue. Said one, "The American invents as the Greek chiselled, as the Venetian painted, as the modern Italian sings."[37] This inventiveness was referred to as self-reliance and self-help. It is not to be confused with later interpretations which make self-help a relentless, individual pursuit of gain.

It was mentioned above that the pioneer farmer had many different types of work to perform. Not merely agricultural work but a great deal of manufacturing had to be attended to. In spite of this observers did not witness any excessive industriousness, as the observers understood industriousness. Gersham Flagg, referring to the Illinois settlers, said, "The people of this territory are from all parts of the United States and do the least work, I believe, of any people in the world."[38] Woods in his *English Prairie,* referring to the same people, qualified his observation. "Many of them," he said, "are sometimes truly industrious, and at other times excessively idle. Numbers of them can turn their hands to many things; having been accustomed to do for themselves in small societies."[39]

James Hall mentioned the slovenliness with which things were done and the apparent shiftlessness of the population. "The traveler," he said, "accustomed to different modes of life, is struck with the crude and uncomfortable appearance of everything about this people—the rudeness of their habitations, the carelessness of their agriculture, the unsightly coarseness of all their implements and furniture, the unambitious homeliness of all their goods and chattels. . . ."[40] Not that industriousness was unknown; work was enjoined on all members of the community.[41] But only at certain times. Certain work required the strength of more than one. Since labor was scarce and hired laborers almost unknown neighbors were expected to assist. One who was too enterprising in pushing his own cultivation and did not have time to assist others was considered an undesirable member of the community. Furthermore, he might discover that his own appeals for assistance went unheeded unless he observed the practice of assisting others. Excessive enterprise and industry were rather pointless anyhow since there was no nearby market in which the surplus production could be sold. In this situation the farmers considered neighborliness and generosity rather than industry and enterprise the true economic virtues.

The religious denominations that were particularly strong on the frontier expressed economic virtues to some extent. In part the virtues preached by the pioneer preachers reflected the other-worldly emphasis in some of the religion of the time and in part reflected actual frontier life.

The Methodists were particularly successful on the frontier. In 1800 there were 2,622 white and 179 negro members of the Methodist church in the entire Western country. Twelve years later the numbers had grown to 29,093 white and 1,648 negro members.[42] The only other denomination comparable to the Methodist in size and influence was the Baptist.[43] The Anglicans, Congregationalists, and Presbyterians were much less successful on the frontier.[44]

The success of these groups is sometimes explained by saying these denominations appealed to the frontiersman's love for democracy and individualism.[45] These qualities played a small rôle in the successful churches. Consider the methods by which success was attained. The preaching that increased the number of converts was evangelical and stressed deep emotion.[46] The camp meeting was a convenient means of bringing large numbers of people under the influence of the gospel. And under the influence of exhortation and singing the emotion of a few spread to the entire crowd. Many were converted at the meetings. If the camp meeting had been the sole means of propagating the gospel increased membership would not have been assured, since many converts had a habit of slipping back into sin. The minister could not completely safeguard the new members against evil influences. The minister was usually a circuit rider and found it difficult to make regular visits to all the churches. This difficulty was largely overcome in the Methodist church by such organizations as the class-meeting, the "love feast," and watch services. These were all means by which the members and new converts strengthened one another's faith. A class had ten members who met regularly, testified regarding their own faith, encouraged the less devout, and frequently became the instrument for the conversion of others. The class meetings were connected with an individual church. A number of churches were joined into what was called an Annual Conference. After 1808 all of the Annual Conferences elected delegates to the General Conference, which met every four years and was the governing body of the entire church. This seems like a republican form of organization but the General Conference kept a close control on the Annual Conferences and individual churches. A Bishop presided over the Annual Conferences and was the sole interpreter of the laws and rules of the General Conference. If the Annual Conference did not like the decisions of the Bishop they could appeal to the next General Conference, which might or might not agree to their requests. Individual freedom was not conspicuous in such a system. The individual was controlled by the class-meeting, the class-meeting by the church, the church by the Annual Conference, and the Annual Conference by the General Conference. Under such an organization individual waywardness was quickly checked. The pressure of the group kept many individuals in line when they could easily have lost their religion if the pressure had not been present.

Such doctrines as were preached by the Methodists had an individualistic slant but their observance was enforced by collective effort. All men were conceived and born in sin and Christ died for all. Each individual was responsible for his own salvation. In order that he might attain it he was endowed with free will. Spiritual regeneration was to be attained by conversion. These doctrines were not logically followed. Few individuals attained regeneration in isolation or by relying on their own efforts. Many of the pioneers were hardened and obdurate sinners. They had to be "prayed through," that is, they were assisted to the light by the pleas, prayers, and exhortations of the saved. Nor is it accurate to say that the doctrines developed as a response to frontier life. John Wesley had made the process of regeneration an individual experience long before there was any thought of frontier life or conditions.

Conversion was not the end of religious experience. It was the beginning. The individual was to reveal the "Fruit of the

Spirit." Certain behavior was expected of him that would distinguish him from the sinful. Nominally these good works consisted of: observance of the Sabbath, reverence for the sacred name of Deity, strict justice in dealing, obedience to lawful authority, and fraternal conduct.[47] In preaching the Methodists emphasized certain traits that were thought marks of other-worldliness, such as, equality, temperance, hard work, frugality, and plainness of living and dress.[48]

Some of these other-worldly virtues fitted in very nicely with aspects of frontier life. Take the matter of equality. There was little specialization of labor on the frontier, with the result that one individual could do a number of tasks about as well as any one else in the community. He was frequently requested to do so regardless of his position. This led to a sameness of techniques learned and work done. In religion salvation was open to all, but no special privileges exempted one from the experience. All must be converted and all in about the same way. The equality in this case overruled individual freedom. As in other societies freedom consisted in doing what every one else was doing. If one's behavior varied from the norm then equality was appealed to. Since all were thought to be equal then every one must have the same experience. No exceptions were made. The much quoted experience of Peter Cartwright, one of the pioneer preachers, with General Andrew Jackson illustrates the way equality was sometimes applied. Cartwright was preaching in Nashville when General Jackson entered the church. The presiding minister warned Cartwright of the General's presence. Cartwright replied in an audible voice, "Who is General Jackson? If he don't get his soul converted, God will damn him as quick as he would a Guinea negro!"[49] The Methodists were pleased with this sally.

Frugality, parsimony, temperance, and industriousness were emphasized not because they were economic virtues but because they were considered manifestations of other-worldliness. Wesley had said, "Friendship with the world is spiritual adultery." But as the Methodist church developed in England its members rose in the economic scale. As H. R. Niebuhr expresses it the

Methodist denomination changed from a church of the disinherited to a church of the middle class. This forced some adjustment to the question of money making. Wesley voiced the difficulty as well as his solution to the problem. - He said:

Wherever riches have increased the essence of religion has decreased in the same proportion. Therefore I do not see how it is possible in the nature of things for any revival of religion to continue long. For religion must necessarily produce both industry and frugality, and these cannot but produce riches. But as riches increase so will pride, anger, and love of the world in all its branches. . . . We ought not to prevent people from being diligent and frugal; we must exhort all Christians to gain all they can, and to save all they can; that is in effect to grow rich. What way then can we take, that our money may not sink us into the nethermost hell? There is one way and there is no other under Heaven. If those who gain all they can, and save all they can, will likewise give all they can, then the more they gain, the more they will grow in grace, and the more treasures they will lay up in heaven.[50]

This difficulty had not developed on the frontier in America simply because the members of the Methodist church were not yet living in a society where money making was a recognized institution. At a later time they found money making a most satisfactory means of "growing in grace," but while they were pioneer farmers and not accustomed to buying and selling commodities and labor they did not think of frugality and industry as leading to wealth. In fact, they thought these traits would prevent the acquisition of wealth and its corrupting influence. Plain living and frugality were expected to set the Methodists apart from the more prosperous business groups that were appearing in the West.

Cartwright's reflections on a day that was past illustrate the. emphasis placed on frugality and plainness of living and dress. He said:

The Methodists in that early day dressed plain; attended their meetings faithfully, . . . they wore no jewelry, no ruffles. . . . They religiously kept the Sabbath day; many of them abstained from dram drinking, not because the temperance

movement was ever heard of in that day, but because it was inter-
dicted in the General Rules of our Discipline. . . . Parents did
not allow their children to go to balls or plays; they did not send
them to dancing schools; they generally fasted once a week, and
almost universally on the Friday before each quarterly meeting.
If the Methodists had dressed in the same "superfluity of naughti-
ness" then as they do now, there were very few even out of the
church that would have had any confidence in their religion. But
O, how things have changed in this educational age of the
world![51]

While such practices were advocated for their presumed
value in encouraging other-worldliness the farming frontier was
such as to make the practices of these virtues possible. There was
relatively slight contact with commercial and business life as now
understood.[52] Money was scarce. The farmers did not buy and
sell commodities or labor, although they exchanged them with
their neighbors.[53] The preachers' admonitions to refrain from
money making and to practice frugality were not difficult to
observe under such conditions.

The preachers considered money the source of all evil and
when commercial groups began to spread through the West, or
rather when the preachers came into contact with them, an easy
explanation was found for all sorts of "wickedness."

A Methodist minister who visited Wisconsin in 1835 said of
some of the towns: "Infidelity triumphed, and religion had but
a nominal existence. Add to this, the spirit of money making
seemed to absorb the whole community. Money was made with
the greatest facility and spent with the greatest profusion; and as
a matter of course, gambling, drunkenness, etc., were the common
order of the day, with the majority."[54] The churches even
objected to a paid clergy lest immorality should spread. Schermer-
horn, on a trip through the West, observed that, "against the
salaries of ministers they (the Baptists) are clamorous, and they
denominate Presbyterian ministers as 'fleecers of the flock.' . . .
The manner of the Methodist preaching very much resembles
that of the Baptists; is very controversial and most bitter against
Calvinists. They rail very much against the practice of the Presbyterians receiving pay for preaching, calling them hirelings."[55]

The Methodists suggested that wealth and virtue were incompatible. The attitude is illustrated in a dialogue called Happiness in a Cottage which appeared in the Methodist Magazine and Review for 1837.[56]

MRS. RANDALL: "But surely, Mr. Villiers, you do not mean that the possession of a competent income is sinful, nor that it is a crime to enjoy the elegances of life, provided it be done with moderation and pious gratitude."

MR. VILLIERS: "I cheerfully admit, madam, that in the mere possession of wealth or its accompaniments there is not absolutely any sin, and yet, when the possession so often leads to the abuse; when riches have so strong a tendency to attach us to the world, to nurture our pride, to unfit us for spiritual duties, and to undermine our sacred principles: ought we to consider the possession of them so very desirable, or their absence so great an evil?"

This advice could be followed without calling for any great renunciation of worldly goods since the worldly goods were few in number. Frontier life could be interpreted in a way that would fit in with the other-worldly virtues. Daniel Drake, in referring to his own training on the frontier, said, "I was preserved from many temptations and practically taught self-denial, because indulgence beyond certain narrow limits was so much out of the question as not to be thought of. I was taught the value of time, by having more to do day after day than could be well accomplished. I was taught to practice economy, and to think of money as a thing not to be expended on luxuries but to be used for useful ends."[57] The books he read were the Bible, *Pilgrim's Progress, Æsop's Fables,* Franklin's *Life, The Prompter* (moral homilies on conduct), and *The Life of Robinson Crusoe.* The reading of such books was expected to increase the practice of parsimony, frugality, and industriousness. The aim was to encourage people to live on what they had by parsimony and thrift. The intention was not to encourage them to increase their incomes or get ahead by accumulating property.

Self-help and individual enterprise can be discovered among the pioneers and farmers on the frontier. But these terms have to be taken in terms of the frontier life rather than in terms of later developments. In the frontier community, where a shortage of labor and little specialization existed, individual activity was subordinated to cooperative and collective activity. In this situation a "good" man was one willing to assist in collective activities. Within the collective activity there was plenty of room and necessity for individual effort. But it was the neighborliness that became virtuous behavior rather than the work connected with one's own land.

Furthermore, the necessity of doing a number of different tasks made it difficult to concentrate on any one. Hence observers detected a lack of industriousness. The frontiersmen were continually going from one task to another or else waiting for assistance with their work.

Their restlessness and mobility would not seem to be either a mark of independence or of enterprise. Restlessness started when settlement increased. The new and strange society growing up about them frightened them away. Their departure might be interpreted as love of adventure. More plausibly it would seem to be inertia and habituation to a certain type of life.

Individual variations among the pioneers were slight. The sameness of the conditions under which they lived and lack of specialization made one man's behavior very much like another's. Too great individuality was not tolerated.

The religious influence emphasized frugality and industry because of their presumed other-worldliness. Individual salvation was preached. In practice even this individualism was frequently overshadowed by co-operative activity. Frugality and industry were combined with neighborliness as representing virtuous behavior.

Such industry, frugality and thrift as was preached and practiced was not supposed to lead to great wealth. These virtues were recommended because they were thought to prevent any such outcome. From the farmers' point of view licentiousness, dishonesty and prodigality were characteristics of the wealthy. The farmers thought that industry, frugality and thrift had nothing to do with acquiring great wealth.

FOOTNOTES FOR CHAPTER I

[1] E. C. Semple, *The Influence of Geographic Environment*, ch. 7.

[2] F. J. Turner, *The Frontier in American History, passim*.

[3] *Ibid.* Also, F. J. Turner, *The Rise of the New West*, p. 107.

[4] T. Roosevelt, *The Winning of the West*. Vol. 4, p. 224.

[5] C. L. Becker, in *Essays in American History Dedicated to F. J. Turner*, p. 89.

[6] V. L. Parrington, *Main Currents in American Thought*. Vol. 2, "The Romantic Revolution in America," p. vi, pp. 162-166.

[7] W. H. Macleod, *The American Indian Frontier*, p. 368.

[8] C. W. Alvord, *The Daniel Boone Myth*, Illinois State Historical Society Journal. Vol. 19, pp. 16-30.

[9] R. G. Thwaites, *Early Western Travels*. Vol. 3, pp. 194ff., quotation from F. A. Michaux's "Travels," 1802.

[10] J. M. Peck, *A New Guide for Emigrants to the West*, pp. 119ff., as quoted in F. J. Turner, *The Frontier in American History*, pp. 19ff. Also, Callot, *Journey in North America*, p. 109.

[11] S. J. Buck, *Illinois in 1818*, pp. 98ff.

[12] T. C. Pease, *The Frontier State, 1818-1848*, p. 6.

[13] A. T. Volwiler, *Croghan and the Westward Movement*, pp. 233-259.

[14] J. R. Commons, ed., *Documentary History of American Industrial Society*. Vol. 2, "The Founding of Louisville, Ky."

[15] W. P. Shortridge, *Transition of a Typical Frontier, passim*.

[16] J. Doddridge, *Notes on the Settlement and Indian Wars of the Western Parts of Virginia and Pennsylvania from 1736 to 1783*, pp. 58-59.

[17] Buck, *op. cit.*, pp. 97-98.

[18] Commons, ed., *op. cit.*, vol. 2, p. 256.

[19] J. M. Peck, *Forty Years of Pioneer Life*, p. 145.

[20] M. Birkbeck, *Notes on a Journey in America, from the Coast of Virginia to the Territory of Illinois*, pp. 106, 110.

[21] Macleod, *op. cit.*, p. 372.

[22] Parrington, *op. cit.*, p. 179.

[23] Doddridge, *op. cit.*, pp. 37-38. Also, Peck, *Forty Years of Pioneer Life*, p. 137. Also, S. P. Hildreth, *Original Contributions to the "American Pioneer,"* pp. 10ff., 95.

[24] Macleod, *op. cit.*, pp. 228-229.

[25] W. B. Stevens, *Missourians One Hundred Years Ago*, p. 24. Also, *Missouri Historical Review*. Vol. 3, pp. 52ff., 99ff.

[26] C. Schultz, Jr., *Travels on an Inland Voyage*. Vol. 2, p. 55. Also, M. M. Quaife, *Chicago and the Old Northwest, 1673-1835*, pp. 18ff.

[27] W. C. Howells, *Recollections of Life in Ohio, 1813-1840*, p. 154.

[28] Howells, *op. cit.*, p. 146. See the following for examples of this and other collective activity: R. King, *Ohio*, pp. 298ff.; "Pioneer Life," *Indiana Magazine of History*. Vol. 3, pp. 4ff.; "Recollections of Pioneer Life in Mississippi," *Mississippi Historical Society Publication*. Vol. 4, pp. 344ff.; *Illinois State Historical Society Transactions*, 1905, p. 54.

[29] "Farm Life in Central Ohio," *Western Reserve Historical Society Tracts*. Vol. 4, No. 86, p. 32.

[30] T. Ford, *History of Illinois, 1818-1847*, pp. 41-42. Also, J. Hall, *The Romance of Western History, or Sketches of History, Life and Manners in the West*. Vol. 2, pp. 68-69.

[31] D. Drake, *Pioneer Life in Kentucky*, in *Ohio Valley Historical Series*, No. 6, pp. 17ff.

[32] Tryon, *Household Manufactures in the United States*, p. 118. For description of pioneer industry in the West, see *Journal of Political Economy*. Vol. 18, "Pioneer Industry in the West," by Lippincott.

[33] Buck, *op., cit.*, p. 130.

[34] J. Hall, *op. cit.*, p. 68.

[35] T. Ford, *op. cit.*, pp. 41-42.

[36] G. G. Goodrich, *Recollections of a Lifetime*. Vol. 1, p. 90.

[37] W. M. West, *The Story of American Democracy*, p. 352.

[38] Buck, *op. cit.*, p. 163.

[39] Thwaites, *op. cit.*, vol. 10, p. 317. Also, *Journal of Political Economy*. Vol. 18, article by Lippincott, p. 277.

[40] J. Hall, *op. cit.*, p. 70.

[41] Howells, *op. cit.*, p. 154. Also, Thwaites, *op. cit.*, vol. 9, pp. 92-93.

[42] W. W. Sweet, *The Rise of Methodism in the West*, p. 35. Also, *Mississippi Valley Historical Review*. Vol. 15, No. 1, pp. 69-88, "Rise of Methodism in the Middle West."

[43] Pease, *op. cit.*, pp. 262-263. Also, Stevens, *op. cit.*, p. 16. Also, J. L. Mesick, *The English Traveller in America, 1785-1835*, pp. 262-263. Also, H. R. Niebuhr, *The Social Sources of Denominationalism*, ch. 7.

[44] Niebuhr, *op. cit.*, ch. 6.

[45] Roosevelt, *op. cit.*, vol. 4, p. 248.

[46] *Mississippi Valley Historical Review*. Vol. 15, p. 82.

[47] *Methodist Quarterly Review*. Vol. 39, pp. 28off., "Influence of Methodism upon the Civilization and Education of the West," by Eddy.

[48] Thwaites, *op. cit.*, vol. 10, p. 129. Also, Roosevelt, *op. cit.*, vol. 4, p. 249. Also, Sweet, *op. cit.*, pp. 62-63. Also, Buck, *op. cit.*, pp. 173ff. Also *Methodist Quarterly Review*. Vol. 53, p. 581, "Early Methodism in the West."

[49] Sweet, *op. cit.*, p. 14.

[50] Quoted in Niebuhr, *op. cit.*, pp. 70-71.

[51] *Methodist Review*. Vol. 55, pp. 83-84.

[52] *Illinois State Historical Society Transactions, 1905*, p. 40.

[53] Buck, *op. cit.*, p. 140. Also, *Indiana Magazine of History*. Vol. 3, p. 125, and vol. 10, p. 26.

[54] *Wisconsin Historical Collections*. Vol. 15, p. 287, "Methodist Circuit Rider's Tour from Pennsylvania to Wisconsin, 1835."

[55] *Illinois State Historical Society Transactions*, 1905, p. 305, "Puritan Influences," by Kofoid.

[56] *Methodist Magazine and Review*. Vol. 19, pp. 273ff., "Happiness in a Cottage."

[57] Drake, *op. cit.*, pp. 87ff.

CHAPTER II

THE GROWTH OF BUSINESS IN THE WEST

AFTER the War of 1812 the population of the middle West increased rapidly. Before the war immigration from Europe had been at the rate of some four or five thousand people a year. In 1817 the number of immigrants rose at a bound to 22,000, and most of these went immediately to the West. Many Easterners sought relief from the business depression of 1816-1820 by striking out for the West. Morris Birkbeck wrote in 1817: "Old America seems to be breaking up. We are seldom out of sight, as we travel this grand track toward the Ohio, of family groups before or behind us." During the decade 1820-1830 the Western states grew at the rate of from one hundred to a hundred and fifty per cent, while Massachusetts and Virginia remained almost stationary. "New England had sent many settlers into western New York and Ohio; the Western Reserve had increased in population by the immigration of Connecticut people; Pennsylvania and New Jersey had sent colonists to southern and central Ohio, with Cincinnati as the commercial center."[1] In Ohio the settlers of middle state origin were more numerous than those from the South, and those from the South were more numerous than the New Englanders.[2] The great bulk of immigrants from the South were the poorer whites, the more democratic, non-slave holding people from the southern uplands. Many, if not most, of these immigrants became settlers and farmers. A good many of the others also settled on the land and lived in a manner not greatly different from that described in the preceding chapter. But with this large number of immigrants came many who were primarily merchants and speculators. Numbers of these settled in towns and followed a type of economic activity that was quite strange to the farmers.

Those who were primarily business men were not accustomed to frontier self-sufficiency. They were in the habit of

buying what they needed, and they brought the money with which
to pay for it.[3] Ford in his *History of Illinois* noted some of the
changes that followed in the wake of this new population :[4]

Upon the conclusion of the War of 1812 the people from the
old states began to come in and settle in the country. They
brought some money and some property with them, and introduced some changes in the customs and modes of living. Before
the war such a thing as money was scarcely ever seen in the country, the skins of the deer and the raccoon supplying the place of
a circulating medium. The money which was now brought in,
and which had before been paid by the United States to the
militia during the war, turned the heads of all the people, and gave
them new ideas and aspirations; so that by 1819 the whole country was in a rage for speculating in lands and town lots. The
states of Ohio and Kentucky, a little before, had each incorporated
a batch of about forty independent banks. The Illinois territory
had incorporated two at home, one at Edwardsville and the other
at Shawneetown; and the territory of Missouri added two more
at Saint Louis. These banks made money very plenty; emigrants
brought it to the state in great abundance. The owners had to
use it in some way; and as it could not be used in legitimate commerce in a state where the material for commerce did not exist,
the most of it was used to build houses in towns which the limited
business of the country did not require, and to purchase land
which the labor of the country was not sufficient to cultivate.
This was called "developing the infant resources of a new country."

Land speculation was one of the means of developing towns
and cities in the West.

In the spring and summer of 1836, the great land and town
lot speculation of those times had fairly reached and spread over
Illinois. It commenced in this state first at Chicago, and was the
means of building up that place in a year or two from a village
of a few houses, to be a city of several thousand inhabitants.
The story of the sudden fortunes made there excited at first
wonder and amazement, next a gambling spirit of adventure, and
lastly, an all-absorbing desire for sudden and splendid wealth.
Chicago has been for some time only one great town market.
The plats of towns for one hundred miles around, were carried
there to be disposed of at auction. . . .

The example of Chicago was contagious. It spread to all

the towns and villages of the state. New towns were laid out in every direction. The number of towns multiplied so rapidly, that it was waggishly remarked by many people, that the whole country was likely to be laid out into towns; and that no land would be left for farming purposes. The judgments of all our business men were unsettled, and their minds occupied only by the one idea, the all-absorbing desire of jumping into a fortune.[5]

Not only were the towns largely started by speculators but they were inhabited by speculators who bought lots and settled down to the real estate business hoping that an increased population would increase the value of their holdings.

Some of the towns were not merely speculative centers; they were also centers of commerce, industry, and trade. Pittsburgh, Cincinnati, Marietta, Vincennes, Saint Louis, and New Orleans were important shipping centers or distributing centers for manufactured goods.

Under the influence of the type of population gathered in the towns almost the entire community was devoted to the goal of money-making. Even the professional people in the towns hoped to amass a fortune in one way or another. In many of the towns "the most universal occupation was trading and speculating in land. Nearly every man of capital or credit was buying or trading town lots or farm land."[6] The lawyers took up the same business-like interest in the community. An Albany attorney who was considering settling in the West wrote to a friend in Illinois, "Can an attorney expect to succeed without Some capital to embark in Speculations, and what is the Smallest Sum which will be requisite? . . . I have . . . from one to two thousand dollars. Will such funds justify the adventure?"[7] Politicians as well as the lawyers were interested in speculation.[8]

This interest in speculation led to a roseate view of the country's future. Timothy Flint referred to the West as a land of "puffers." Pessimism and indifference would not sell land. He said, "Art and ingenuity have been exhausted in devising new ways of alluring purchasers to take lots and build in the new town."[9] The salesman and booster was at a premium.

G. A. Worth, who visited Cincinnati in 1820-21, described one of these enterprising business men:

> Mr. Glenn possessed, in an eminent degree, the qualities that in those days characterized a great majority of the landholders and gentlemen traders of the West—qualities that might be stereotyped, as applicable to nearly all, and as forming a part of the character of each. These qualities, if I may venture to name them, were confidence in the increasing value of their lands, growing out of the tide of emigration which was then setting strongly in; a self-appreciation, arising from the consciousness of the fact that they had made themselves what they were; a frankness and an unceremonious cordiality of manner, the natural offspring of ease and independence; a hospitality, unequalled in any other part of the Union, springing in the first place from necessity, and continued from a sense of its liberality and dignity, until it became in time the law of the land; a spirit of enterprise, a disposition to go ahead and make a fortune; a readiness to embark in large and hazardous operations, with borrowed means, or even with no means at all. To these may be added a disregard for trifles—by which they meant anything short of positive ruin; and a sovereign contempt for prudence and small change! By the latter was understood any sum under five thousand dollars! It is hardly necessary to add to these, the then invariable characteristic of a Western gentleman, a high sense of honor, which was, in many cases, better than his bond.[10]

Mr. Glenn's frankness, generosity, hospitality, and unceremoniousness were qualities not unknown on the rural frontier. His type of enterprise was a new phenomenon for the hunters and farmers. Other traits appeared that had been poorly cultivated by the hunters and farmers.

Those devoted to money-making made much more display of industriousness than had the rural populations. Travelers were impressed by the diligence with which the townspeople pushed their trades. F. J. Grund, who traveled in the United States in 1836, was greatly impressed by this businesslike aspect of the Americans. He said:

> There is, probably, no people on earth with whom business constitutes pleasure, and industry amusement, in an equal degree with the inhabitants of the United States of America. Active

occupation is not only the principal source of their happiness, and the foundation of their national greatness, but they are absolutely wretched without it, and instead of the *"dolce far niente,"* know but the horrors of idleness. Business is the very soul of an American: he pursues it, not as a means of procuring for himself and his family the necessary comforts of life, but as the fountain of all human felicity; and shows as much enthusiastic ardor in his application to it as any crusader ever evinced for the conquest of the Holy Land, or the followers of Mohammed for the spreading of the Koran.

From the earliest hour in the morning till late at night, the streets, offices, and warehouses of the large cities are thronged by men of all trades and professions, each following his vocation like a perpetuum mobile, as if he never dreamed of cessation from labor, or the possibility of becoming fatigued. If a lounger should happen to be parading the street, he would be sure to be jostled off the sidewalk, or to be pushed in every direction, until he keeps time with the rest. Should he meet a friend, he will only talk to him on business; on 'change they will only hear him on business. Wherever he goes, the hum and bustle of business will follow him; and when he finally sits down to his dinner, hoping there, at least, to find an hour of rest, he will discover, to his sorrow, that the Americans treat that as a business too, and despatch it in less time than he is able to stretch his legs under the mahogany. In a very few minutes the clang of steel and silver will cease, and he will again be left to his solitary reflections, while the rest are about their business. In the evenings, if he have not friends or acquaintances, none will intrude on his retirement; for the people are either at home with their families, or preparing for the business of the next day.

Whoever goes to the United States, for the purpose of settling there, must resolve, in his own mind, to find pleasure in business, and business in pleasure, or he will be disappointed and wish himself back to the sociable idleness of Europe. Nor can anyone travel in the United States without making a business of it. . . . He must resign the gratification of his own individual tastes to the wishes of the majority who are traveling on business, and with whom speed is infinitely more important than all that contributes to pleasure; he must eat, drink, sleep, and wake, when they do, and has no other remedy for the catalogue of his distresses but the hope of their speedy termination. . . .

Machines are invented, new lines of communication established, and the depths of the sea explored to afford scope for the spirit of enterprise; and it is as if all America were but one gigantic workshop, over the entrance of which there is the blazing inscription "No admission here, except on business."[11]

While the enterprise and industriousness of the business groups was becoming obvious, these traits were not thought of as economic virtues—at least not yet. New virtues were not immediately developed. Many of the Western men were out to make a fortune, and they did not worry whether or not their behavior was of the approved variety! The speculators, in acquiring land, endeavored not only to secure their legitimate share, but also all they could lay their hands on, legally or otherwise. They were highly successful, and the policies they pursued in the acquisition of land were commonly accepted and seemed to have wide social approval.[12] They did not feel that honesty was necessarily the best policy or that frugality and wise economy were necessary to make money.

The early storekeepers, traders, and merchants were not outstanding exemplars of the homely virtues of thrift, prudence, and honesty. Thomas Ashe described the business methods of the storekeepers as follows:

These storekeepers are obliged to keep every article which it is possible that the farmer and manufacturer may want. Each of their shops exhibits a complete medley. . . . As farmers and manufacturers advance in business, and find their produce more than equal to the wants of their families, they contract with the storekeeper to receive the annual balance of the latter, either in cash or in land to an equal amount; for though no person cultivates a tenth part of the land he possesses, every one is animated with the rage of making further accessions. Thus the great landholders ultimately absorb all the hard money; and as they principally reside in the large towns on the Atlantic States, the money finds its way back to those, and leaves many places here without a single dollar. This is productive of distressing incidents to small farmers who supply the markets with provisions; for whatever they have to sell, whether trivial or important, they receive nothing in return but an order on a store for the value in goods; and as the wants of such persons are few, they seldom know what articles to take. The storekeepers turn this circumstance to advantage, and frequently force on the customer a thing for which he has no use; or what is worse, when the order is trifling, tell him to sit down at the door and drink the amount if he chooses. As this is often complied with, a market day is mostly a scene of drunkenness and contention, fraud, cunning, and duplicity; the storekeeper denying the possession of a good article, till he fails in imposing a bad one. I have known a person ask for a pair of shoes, and receive for answer that there were no shoes in the store, but some capital gin that could be recommended to him. I have heard another ask for a rifle gun, and be answered that there were no rifles, but that he could be accommodated with the best Dutch looking glasses and German flutes in the Western country.[13]

The merchants received considerable opposition from the farmers. The farmers were not accustomed to producing for a market outside their control. Some of them solved the problem by moving farther West. Those who remained attempted to protect themselves by increased efforts at self-sufficiency. "Our corn we must not neglect under the penalty of starving," said one of the farmers. "The attitude of this man seems to have been the prevalent one at that time in Illinois (1818); each and all raised produce not primarily to sell, but to save themselves from being obliged to buy. . . ."[14] They continued to "trade, barter, and exchange commodities and swap work in corn-planting time, for work back in corn-husking and hay-making time."[15] This was about the only commerce known to them. Their greatest economic difficulties came when they had to pay cash for things. "Those who had payments to make on their land were pretty sure to sell themselves bare, and were often hard put to it to maintain themselves in provisions."[16]

The business groups thought their own material welfare depended on breaking down the self-sufficiency of the farmer. The speculator could get higher prices for land if the population increased and the merchant's profits would mount only if the farmer had greater surplus to exchange for manufactured goods from the East. Apparently the business men were interested in such traits of behavior as would lead to greater interdependence of economic groups.

The storekeepers intensively advertised to get the farmers

into the stores and perhaps were slightly effective in increasing the demands of the farmers for manufactured goods.[17] The example of the speculator and his buoyant optimism brought some change in the economic aspirations of the farmers. The hope of great wealth enticed some of them into the towns.[18] But the change in the farmers' life and attitudes was relatively slight. They attempted to maintain their self-sufficiency, and be "Independent Farmers." The industry, frugality, and neighborliness they preached were means by which they hoped to attain this goal. They attempted to make all economic virtues synonymous with those of the farming communities.[19] The farmers were yet the most influential class in society. They maintained that equality and independence could not be maintained apart from ownership and cultivation of the soil. Factories would demoralize American life by creating a class of wage-earners. Money-making would develop avarice.[20]

The rural population was inclined to agree with Thomas Jefferson that "the cultivators of the earth are the most valuable citizens. They are the most vigorous, the most independent, the most virtuous, and they are tied to their country and wedded to its liberty and interests by the most lasting bonds." Ministers asserted that religion was despised and vilified in the towns, that property holders in the towns opposed it, and that religious societies found their greatest success in the rural areas.[21] The business men did not feel that the farmers' morality was a prerequisite to financial success. One mark of failure was to reveal the frugality and the parsimony that the farmers glorified. And the business groups did not immediately elaborate their own ideas of economic virtues. Virtue, as yet, was no stepping stone to wealth.

Some of the townspeople, however, felt the farmers' criticisms and assumed the virtues preached by the farmers. Others of the wealthy attended the camp meetings lest their absence call down on them adverse criticism.[22] Virtue was not thought of in connection with money-making. The farmers were still in the ascendancy.

FOOTNOTES FOR CHAPTER II

[1] M. M. West, *American Democracy*, p. 394; F. J. Turner, *The Rise of the New West*, p. 76.

[2] *Ibid.*, p. 76.

[3] S. J. Buck, *Illinois in 1818*, p. 147.

[4] T. Ford, *History of Illinois, 1818-1847*, pp. 43ff.

[5] Ford, *op. cit.*, pp. 181-182, quoted in E. L. Bogart and C. M. Thompson, *Readings in Economic History*, pp. 460-461. Other travelers in the West who noted this speculation in the thirties of the nineteenth century are also quoted in Bogart and Thompson, pp. 458-463.

[6] *Mississippi Valley Historical Review*. Vol. 9, No. 4, p. 273, "Old Franklin, A Frontier Town of the Twenties."

[7] *Chicago Historical Society MSS.* Vol. 52, p. 179, quoted in Buck, *op. cit.*, pp. 159-160.

[8] American Economic Association, *Economic Studies.* Vol. 1, p. 155.

[9] T. Flint, *Recollections of the Last Ten Years*, p. 187.

[10] G. A. Worth, *Random Recollections of Albany*, p. 74, "Recollections of Cincinnati 1817-1821."

[11] F. J. Grund, *The Americans.* Vol. 2, pp. 202-204.

[12] R. T. Hill, *The Public Domain and Democracy*, p. 150.

[13] *Travels in America*, pp. 52-53, quoted in W. W. Jennings, *A History of Economic Progress in the United States.*

[14] Buck, *op. cit.*, p. 129.

[15] *Illinois State Historical Society Transactions, 1905*, p. 40.

[16] W. C. Howells, *Recollections of Life in Ohio, 1813-1840*, p. 122.

[17] Buck, *op. cit.*, pp. 147-148.

[18] J. Reynolds, *My Own Times, Embracing also the History of My Life*, pp. 77, 284.

[19] American Economic Association, *Economic Studies.* Vol. 1, pp. 133-209. Also, A. D. Jones, *Illinois and the West*, pp. 67-68.

[20] J. L. Mesick, *The English Traveller in America, 1785-1835*, pp. 151, 165.

[21] J. M. Peck, *Forty Years of Pioneer Life*, p. 87. Also, F. C. Holliday, *History of Indiana Methodism*, pp. 97-98.

[22] T. Flint, *The History and Geography of the Mississippi Valley*, p. 144.

CHAPTER III

PURITANISM AND MONEY-MAKING

MONEY-MAKING in the West was without the pale of virtuous behavior. Economic virtues were associated with farm life; vice was associated with commercial and business activity. But the business groups in the towns were increasing and commercial activity could no longer be considered a temporary perversion. Furthermore, the New England immigrants were not uninfluenced by Puritanism. The result was that a religious sanction, formerly confined to farming, began to develop for business. The New England immigrants tended to concentrate in the Western towns. The settlers from the Southern states predominated in the rural areas.[1] Not only did the New Englanders settle in the towns but they came in sufficiently large numbers to preserve their traditions as to what was fit and proper economic activity. For example, Granville, Ohio, was founded by a colony of one hundred and seventy-six persons who emigrated from Granville, Mass. They brought their town organization, their Congregational church, and their plans for founding a college with them.[2] The group was large enough to protect itself from the contaminating influence of the rude Westerners and incidentally spread its own doctrine of economic virtues.

To observe the manner in which they connected economic virtues with money-making it is necessary to consider the influence of Puritanism.

Puritanism has interested economic historians on account of its presumed influence on economic behavior. There have been attempts to explain capitalism (at least the Capitalistic Spirit) by referring to various Puritan teachings. It is not necessary to go into this controversy to indicate the relationship between the economic virtues and Puritanism. Puritanism did not create certain economic virtues since the same type of behavior was considered virtuous in societies untouched by Puritanism, for example in

fifteenth-century Florence.[3]   Nor did Puritanism necessarily
justify free private enterprise.   There was very little free enterprise under Calvin's government at Geneva.   Man's life, includ-
ing his economic affairs, was regulated by the leaders of the church
and their authority derived from the scriptures properly interpreted.   Nor could the church members control God's representatives, that is, the ministers.   Calvin himself greatly distrusted the
abilities of the ordinary man and abhorred democracy.[4]

For a time in New England under the Theocracy the same
sort of government prevailed.   The church decided that certain
activities should be prohibited.   Completely free economic enterprise was not recognized.   Forestalling, engrossing, and regrating were prohibited while the Theocracy was in the ascendancy.[5]
Laws were passed attempting to establish wages and prices.   There
was an attempt to abolish certain "false economic principles"
such as the one that "a man might sell as dear as he can and buy as
cheap as he can."   And laws against idleness were passed in 1636
and again in 1682.[6]

The theocratic control over economic affairs did not last
beyond the first two generations of Puritans in New England.[7]
Religious dissensions resulted in either the banishment or withdrawal of some of the members of the community.   Quarrels over
the division of lands in the new towns led to the departure of some
of the dissatisfied who became freehold farmers farther in the
interior.   The opportunities for profits in the whaling and fishing
industries, the shipping trade, the rum trade, and the China trade
led to the at first surreptitious, and later open, breaking of the
prohibitions against individual economic enterprise.[8]   The prohibitions could be maintained as long as the community was small
and there was little business enterprise since the majority of the
population devoted itself to farming.   With the rise of business
and commercial activities the earlier restrictions were difficult to
retain.

The fall of the Theocracy permitted the formal recognition
and approval of a type of economic activity that had already
started, namely, free private enterprise.   This did not take the
form of producing sufficient commodities for one's existence.   It

was a matter of increasing money income. Money-making was not a new phenomenon to many of the New Englanders. The practice was familiar in the society from which they had emigrated. And many of them had come to the New World with the express intention of making a fortune. The opportunity was not immediately available since agricultural activity was imperative and the ascendancy of the clergy restricted the sphere of individual enterprise for a time, but only a short time.

Money-making grew rapidly. Some of the New Englanders were peddlers of wares in the middle and southern colonies. Because they started in this activity before others did and because their activities were strange to the farmers and non-commercial groups they gained an unsavory reputation with the rest of the country. A European traveling in the United States stated that "he (the New Englander) views the world but as one vast exchange, on which he is impelled, both by principle and interest, to overreach his neighbors if he can."[9] Another observer quoted from Matthew Carey's Olive Branch:

"It is within the memory of those over whose chins no razor has ever mowed a harvest, that Yankee and sharper were regarded as nearly synonymous, and this was not among the low, and the illiberal, the base, and the vulgar. It pervaded all ranks of society. In the Middle and Southern states, traders were universally very much on their guard against Yankee tricks, when dealing with those of the Eastern states."

It is therefore in this class of adventurers and emigrants we are to look for the least favorable traits of the New England character: patient, industrious, frugal, enterprising, and intelligent, it cannot be denied, but they are frequently knavish, mean, and avaricious; as men who make gain the master-spring of their actions.[10]

It happened that many of these tradesmen were Puritans. Their devotion to trade was not necessarily created by Puritanism nor did the Puritans invent the economic virtues. There were certain aspects of Puritan teaching that could be admirably adapted to business activity. One of the main emphases in Puritan teaching was to rationalize life; restrain sensual appetites and passions; devote one's self with unwavering fidelity to the accomplishment of a given task.   This attitude is well expressed in Isaac Barrow's treatise "Of Industry":

We should govern and regulate according to very strict and severe laws all the faculties of our soul, all the members of our body, all internal motions and all external actions proceeding from us; we should check our inclinations, curb our appetites, and compose our passions; we should guard our hearts from vain thoughts and bad desires; we should bridle our tongues from evil and from idle discourses; we should order our steps in the straight way of righteousness, not deflecting to the right hand or to the left.[11]

When the Puritans came to the New World they specifically stated that they wanted men whose lives were well controlled and carefully regulated.   They wanted "not men nourished up in idleness, inconstant, and affecting novelties, unwilling, stubborn, inclined to faction, covetous, luxurious, prodigal, but men who were willing, constant, industrious, obedient, frugal, lovers of the common good."[12]   In time the Puritans worshiped the practice of such traits as frugality, thrift and industry without examining the types of occupations in which the virtues were manifested. Money-making was legitimate if the proper virtues accompanied it.

This was important for the development of economic virtues in the Western towns.   As was previously pointed out, the farmers connected virtue with farming life and vice with trading life.   With the Puritan influence money-making was brought within the bounds of respectability.   The Puritans had a habit of making their own behavior synonymous with righteousness. This trait, which has brought down on them so many charges of hypocrisy, became conspicuous in their dealings with the Indians. For example, in 1637 the Puritans from Plymouth discovered an unprotected Indian village containing about four hundred inhabitants and proceeded to set it afire.   Only about five Indians escaped.   The unregenerate, if he were charitable, might interpret this act as a necessary means of self-defense; if he were less charitable he might call it murder.   The Puritans refused to pass any such worldly judgments on their behavior.   Bradford, describing the incident in his *History of Plymouth Plantation,* said,

"It was a fearful sight to see them frying in the fire, and the streams of blood quenching the same, and horrible was the stench and stink thereof. But," he concludes, "the victory seemed a sweet sacrifice and they (the Puritans) gave praise thereof to God." When Mather heard of the incident he entered his pulpit and gave praise to God, thanking him "that on this day we have sent six hundred heathen souls to hell."[13] This method of interpreting their behavior was continued by the Puritans. As will be shown the absorption in business activity was given a religious interpretation and justification. Charges of trickery and knavery in business did not trouble the devout Puritan. He was working for the glory of God, not for the worldly welfare of sinful man.

The Puritan teaching encouraged the development of a type of character that exulted in unceasing absorption in the performance of given tasks. Certain restraints were thrown about man's activity. Certain other types of behavior were considered virtuous because they kept one out of mischief and away from sin. The world was considered a sort of training camp for heaven. Those acts were most virtuous which were calculated to lead one in paths of righteousness. In economic endeavor the virtues were the traditional "middle-class virtues" and were perhaps best expressed in the writings of Benjamin Franklin.

Franklin was not himself a Puritan. He was something of a freethinker, leaning toward the views of the French Deists. He did not recommend certain virtues merely because they led one to righteousness but because they enabled one to get ahead in the world. In the process of getting ahead virtue could develop. The virtues Franklin recommended were the ones the Puritans had already emphasized. The moral instruction of Franklin's Puritan father apparently was influential. Puritan morality is quite evident in Franklin's economic virtues. Max Weber believes that Franklin's homilies represent the result of the application of Puritan teaching to economic life.[14]

Franklin was careful to state that money-making would secure virtue when he explained how he happened to write his "Poor Richardisms." Perhaps he had a Puritan audience in mind. Speaking of his Poor Richard's Almanac, he said:

I considered it a proper vehicle for conveying instruction among the common people, who bought scarcely any other books; I therefore filled all the little spaces that occurred between the remarkable days of the calendar with proverbial sentences, chiefly such as inculcated industry and frugality, as the means of procuring wealth, and thereby securing virtue; it being more difficult for a man in want to act always honestly, as, to use here one of these proverbs, it is hard for an empty sack to stand upright.[15]

He thought that life must be subjected to careful organization and control if one were to make money. Constant attention must be given to prospects to make money and opportunities to save it. No idle diversions should lead one from the constant pursuit of trade. The virtues were to be means by which this goal is attained. He lists thirteen virtues in all: Temperance, Silence, Order, Resolution, Frugality, Industry, Sincerity, Justice, Moderation, Cleanliness, Tranquillity, Chastity, Humility. But there are some more important than others.

In short, the way to wealth, if you desire it, is as plain as the way to market. It depends chiefly on two words, industry and frugality; that is, waste neither time nor money, but make the best use of both. Without industry and frugality nothing will do, and with them everything. He that gets all he can honestly, and saves all he gets (necessary expenses excepted) will certainly become rich, if that Being who governs the world, to whom all should look for a blessing on their honest endeavors, doth not, in His wise providence, otherwise determine.[16]

One should also be prudent. Do nothing that would harm one's credit. In his autobiography Franklin relates his own efforts in this direction:

In order to secure my credit and character as a tradesman I took care not only to be in reality industrious and frugal, but to avoid all appearances to the contrary. I drest plainly; I was seen at no places of idle diversion. I never went out a-fishing or shooting; a book, indeed, sometimes debauched me from my work, but that was seldom, snug and gave no scandal; and to show that I was not above my business, I sometimes brought home the paper I purchased at the stores through the streets on a wheelbarrow. Thus being esteemed an industrious, thriving young man, and paying duly for what I bought, the merchants who imported stationery solicited my custom; others proposed supplying me with books, and I went on swimmingly.[17]

Franklin did not take his own moral maxims too seriously. As one of his biographers says, "before 1732 he had never saved any money; never brought order into his affairs; and never lived either a regular or a moral life."[18] In 1732 Franklin was twenty-five years old and had at last succeeded in the printing business. In 1732 Poor Richard's Almanack was published. This book was to make his fortune. In 1748 Franklin took in a partner and retired from active business the following year. Thereafter the "Poor Richardisms" were not conspicuous in his own behavior.[19]

Though Franklin failed to take his own maxims seriously the Puritans succeeded in doing so. The doctrines suited them admirably. With Poor Richard's maxims they could at once make money and attain a state of grace. Not a few New Englanders distinguished themselves in the practice of prudential morality.[20]

Prudential morality was part of the equipment the Puritans took with them to the West. They felt their duty was to change the Western states from centers of licentiousness to strongholds of righteousness. Not that they were unassisted in this task. Middle class Englishmen emigrated directly to the West and started settlements such as Flower's and Birkbeck's in the Illinois country.[21] They held essentially the same views regarding economic behavior as did the New Englanders. The Quakers who had gone from Pennsylvania into the Southern states migrated to the Middle West in the early nineteenth century.[22] The Quakers violently dissented from many Puritan doctrines. But there was more similarity than difference between the groups when it came to the economic virtues. Money-making was not scorned since many of the wealthy merchants in Philadelphia at the close of the eighteenth century were Quakers.[23] The Quakers were great advocates of frugality, thrift, and industry.[24]

As soon as these groups, particularly the Puritans, arrived in the West they made their presence known. They deplored the "survival of intemperance accompanied with ignorance and indolence" that, they supposed, emanated from the settlers from the

South.[25]   Instead of saying, as the farmers had said, that this laxity in morals was due to money-making, they said it was due to lack of interest in money-making. The moral effects of money-making were pointed out. Mr. Ogden, a Quaker merchant from New Bedford, Mass., found in the mixed population of Ohio

industry, temperance, morality, and love of gain. With a population governed by such habits and principles, the state must necessarily advance in improvements at a rapid rate. This, in turn, excites emulation, and precludes idleness, which generates prodigality and vice. The rich being compelled to labor, find but little time for indulgence in luxury and extravagance; their ostentation is restricted, and industry is made to become a characteristic virtue.[26]

When the habits of the people weren't those described by Ogden the Easterners saw opportunity for missionary effort. Flower, a large landholder in Illinois and the founder of Albion, Ill., wrote:

When I was at Philadelphia a lady of the Society of Friends addressed me most emphatically on the subject (of Western settlement). Wilt thou, friend Flower, take thy family to that infidel and wicked settlement in the Illinois? Thou appearest to be a Christian; how wilt thou answer to thy God for endangering the precious lives of thy dear children? Madam, answered I, my destiny appears to be in the Illinois settlement, and rather than turn from thence on the account you have mentioned, you have furnished me with a forcible argument to proceed.[27]

They felt, as they undertook their missionary endeavors in the West, that the economic condition of the farmers was not a favorable one for the growth of virtue. The farmers were too isolated from the rest of the world. They weren't sufficiently industrious in producing for a distant market. A writer in the Edwardsville, Ill., Spectator (Sept. 18, 1821), said, "The farmer thinks it unnecessary to plant more grain than can be disposed of at home; thus, part of his time passes in inactive languor; but once point to him a market where he may have a sure sale for his produce and every nerve is exerted in the cause of industry."[28] After the desirability of production for sale was indicated, the necessity of virtue for success was mentioned. "It is a happy circumstance," wrote Flower, "that while industry is attended with certain success, vice, drunkenness, and idleness are no better off than in Europe; the effect of this will be to give the virtuous the natural ascendancy over the vicious which they ought always to have."[29]

The farmers did not immediately fall in with the proposals. The first contacts between the two groups brought mutual recriminations. The merchants were trying to increase sales at the General Stores. Occasionally the farmers got into debt and couldn't pay immediately. The merchants claimed an honest man pays his debts and insisted on payment. To pay, the farmers were forced to sell their produce for what it would bring. This was frequently unprofitable. One observer exclaimed, "The farmers indebted to the storekeepers are now forced to sell all their corn at one dollar a barrel, and buy it again for their spring and summer use at five dollars a barrel, a fine profit for the monied merchant."[30] The farmers could not see the virtue of honesty when it got them into such predicaments. They were inclined to interpret such transactions as examples of Yankee guile and trickery. In places where the legal enforcement of payments was difficult the farmer sometimes refused to pay. "If a man can or is disposed to pay, he pays; if not so disposed, or not able, he smiles, and tells you to your face he shall not pay."[31] The merchant called him dishonest.

These conflicts merely reflected the economic habits of the respective groups. The farmer was not used to purchasing things outright. Most of the things he needed he borrowed from neighbors without any formal agreement as to payment or time of return. No written records were kept of such transactions. For a time he could not understand why the same procedure should not govern his transactions with the merchant. The only explanation he could see was that the merchant lacked the virtue of neighborliness. Nor could he see that his failure to pay his obligations was dishonest. He interpreted dishonesty as stealing. And stealing was a matter of claim jumping or horse stealing.[32]

The merchant, on the other side, said the honest man would

observe and fulfill the terms of a contract. The virtue of fore-sight was also connected with making contracts. A contract meant taking thought for the morrow. It made the future less uncertain than it would otherwise be. The farmers dismissed all this "taking thought for the morrow and multiplying mechanical devices to meet it," that is, making contracts, as mere Yankee notions.[33] This feeling was so strong that the farmer frequently objected to "larnin'" on the ground that it would teach him to write and get him into trouble over signing notes.[34]

Save for the Baptist and Methodist emphasis on frugality as a sign of other-worldliness there was little attempt by the farmers to make frugality an economic virtue. To be sure the farming communities had to husband their supplies for the ensu-ing winter, but there was no great incentive to restrict consump-tion of goods in order that the goods might be sold. Markets were not sufficiently developed to make this possible. Many of the townspeople from the East thought that expenditures and consumption should be kept at a minimum in order that income might be conserved. Goods on hand were not merely to be con-sumed, they were possible sources of profit. Farmers were greatly incensed when they stopped at a Yankee's home for dinner and discovered that they were expected to pay for their entertain-ment.[35] The Yankee considered this a proper exercise of thrift and frugality; the farmer interpreted it as undue parsimony and lack of hospitality. The Yankee's parsimony was derived from his interest in money-making. It served a double purpose. As frugality increased the margin between income and expenditure would be increased. Furthermore, a frugal person would not be debauched by idle pleasures, and he would be better able to devote himself to business. The Yankees were greatly shocked by the farmers' "waste and extravagance" of food.[36]

The new population was also introducing a different inter-pretation of industry. Having little specialization, and being obliged to perform a number of different tasks, the farmers could not continuously apply themselves to one task. But the business men thought industry consisted in the continuous appli-cation to money-making. The business men who indulged in land speculation considered their activities in buying lands and holding them for sale at a higher price a fair example of industry. They worked hard at this task and should be adequately rewarded, at least, so they said. The farmers were not convinced. They thought work consisted in the actual cultivation of the soil, even though that cultivation was at times dilatory. Such rewards as were available should go to them. They organized Land Claim Associations to see to it that the land remained in the hands of the settlers and cultivators. The following description illustrates their activities:

In 1839 the first land sale by the government was held in Milwaukee, at which persons from all the southern part of the territory came to secure their land. The terms were that the land was to be sold at auction, but no sale was to be less than $1.25 per acre, and if no one bid more the land was to be struck off to the first bidder. Settlers who had made location and improvements on their lands, fearing speculators would bid them up, held a meeting and resolved to hustle and use harsh measures on anyone who bid beyond the government price on a settler's land. The first morning one man began to bid, but the crowd made it so uncomfortable for him that no one other ventured to bid up, and the men who had made improvements procured their lands at the stipulated price and the sale went off without disturbance.[37]

The speculators suggested that if the farmers would but work harder it would not be necessary to organize associations to control the purchase of land. They might increase their surplus, turn it into money, and do a little speculating themselves. The farmers suggested that if the speculators went to work they would not have to gain a living by gathering in the fruits of other people's industry.[38] The farmers thought the speculators were lazy. And since speculators for the most part lived in towns where education was practiced, the farmers sometimes opposed formal schooling because it was thought to increase laziness. As one farmer put it, "Education made young men proud and lazy; and being unwilling to work, they would live by cheating their neighbors"; that is, they were likely to go into business.[39]

In short, the business groups in the West, particularly under the influence of Puritanism, were advocating such traits as they

thought would increase income. Frugality was thought to decrease expenditure and enable one to give undivided attention to
business. Industry meant continual application to business. This
was not merely physical labor but an unrelenting search for business opportunities. This was to be assisted by foresight through
which one could plan for the future; that is, prepare oneself for
possible price changes. Honesty did not preclude shrewd bar-
gaining or even misrepresentation of things to be sold. Here the
buyer must beware. But an honest man would keep his word and
observe the terms of contracts. Otherwise the business man
would have difficulty in "rationally" making his plans for the
future. The attempt was to reduce life as much as possible to a
cool calculation in terms of dollars and cents. The diffusion of
these virtues was greatly aided by their Puritan affiliations. Before
the Puritans became prominent in the West there was a tendency
to make sin and money-making synonymous. Their influence
seemed to change the situation. Some seemed to feel that religion was necessary for success. A gambler in Saint Louis cried:
"There is no doing as you please now in Saint Louis unless you
are rich. If a man is poor, the devil take him if he has any sin.
Saint Louis has become quite an aristocratic place. Unless one
grows pious, and becomes a hypocrite, you can't get along."[40]

The new economic virtues spread as the newer business population spread through the West. But the new virtues were not
merely applied to business (money-making). There was a tendency to make them general economic virtues that applied to all
classes and sections of the population. This tendency was assisted
by the growth of patriotism or nativism, as it was called.

In the early nineteenth century the Easterners were worried
over the new society that was developing in the West. They
thought if it were allowed to proceed unchecked it might cause
the downfall of "American institutions." It was not until the
forties that the feeling developed into a movement designed to
enforce Americanism and patriotism in the West.[41] As a famous
observer of American life, A. de Tocqueville, noted:

Religious zeal is perpetually stimulated in the United States by the duties of patriotism. . . . They (the Americans) will tell you that "all the American republics are collectively involved with each other; if the republics of the West were to fall into anarchy, or to be mastered by a despot, the republican institutions which now flourish upon the shores of the Atlantic Ocean would be in great peril. It is therefore our interest that the new states should be religious, in order to maintain our liberties."[42]

It turned out that New Englandism, not Americanism, was interesting the down-Easterners. Somehow the two became synonymous. The serious question was: "Could New England morals, religion, and culture flourish on the Western prairies? Would not atheism, radicalism, Catholicism, and intemperance choke Americanism?"

The first cancerous growth on the body politic to engage the attention of the patriots was Catholicism. The Catholics were un-American because they were under allegiance to a foreign sovereign and because there seemed to be a certain looseness and lack of seriousness in their economic and social life. Saint Louis, for example, was founded by French Catholics. It did not become greatly "Americanized" until after about 1830.[43] The Catholic influence persisted and the Eastern Protestants attempted to wipe it out.[44] In doing so, the "Americans" were not merely displacing a form of religion, they were displacing a type of economic activity as well. Saint Louis had developed as a fur trading station from which the French profited. But the French were not enterprising business men as the American interpreted that phenomenon. An early observer said: "They were a contented race of people, patient under hardship, without ambition and ignorant of the prolific resources of the country. . . . They were a frank, open-hearted, joyous people, and careless about the acquisition of property."[45] Nor was this all. Their easy-going life did not call for a strict observance of the Sabbath. Sunday was a day of hilarity, the people gave dances, played cards and billiards. Protestantism along with sobriety, frugality and industry were the remedies proposed for this licentiousness, as it was called.[46]

Another sore spot was the German population. The Germans

emigrated to the United States in great numbers during the forties. The main counts against them were radicalism and a certain lack of Puritanism. They also persisted in using their own language, which frightened some Americans lest a German state be set up within the United States.[47]   There was no objection to them because they lacked all of the proper economic virtues.   Franklin observed at an earlier time that the German immigrants usually surpassed the English in thrift and industry.[48]

These virtues were overshadowed by certain vices that were thought to be alien to the good American.   The New Englanders had frequently asserted that honesty and industry were always accompanied by sobriety, but they discovered that the Germans insisted on their whisky and were not always temperate in its use.[49]   Besides, the Germans had a peculiarly un-American method of Sabbath observance.   While they might go to church, Sunday afternoons were given over to music, dancing, games, and festivities of various kinds.[50]   Other of their characteristics seemed to spring from foreign sources.   Hulme was greatly impressed by the thrift, industry, and wealth of the German community at Harmony on the Wabash.   But all was not for the best in this admirable community.   He said: "I observe that these people are very fond of flowers; by the by, the cultivation of them, and musick, are their chief amusements.   I am sorry to see this, as it is to me a strong symptom of simplicity and ignorance, if not a badge of their German slavery."[51]   No irrelevancies.   Good Americans stick to business.

The Easterners waxed eloquent over these distressing conditions in the West.   They felt irreverence and lawlessness were sweeping over the country.   The only solution was more Puritanism.[52]

The New Englanders continued to identify themselves with real Americanism.   Although New England was in the Mexican War, that disgraceful conflict was really due to the backwoodsmen from the West.   The missionaries from New England in Illinois said, "Shame, indeed, that there should be a Massachusetts and a New England (How art thou fallen from heaven, O Lucifer, son of the morning!) regiment in this war.   But when we look at the hordes which Illinois and Missouri have poured forth, we see where Satan's seat is."[53]

Of course the New Englanders were not able to fit the entire country into their peculiar pattern of "Americanism." But in the process of advancing patriotism they were advancing the . economic virtues encouraged by Puritanism and business activity. They connected these virtues with "Americanism." As will be shown in the following chapter, these virtues were taught in the public schools and were held up as laudable ideals to be practiced by the youth that aspired to distinguish himself in the eyes of his countrymen.

But the economic scene was changing. How did the virtues fare under the new conditions?

FOOTNOTES FOR CHAPTER III

[1] R. W. Patterson, *op. cit.*, p. 105, in Fergus Historical Series, No. 14.

[2] L. K. Mathews, *The Expansion of New England*, p. 180; on the general movement of New Englanders into the Middle West see *ibid.*, ch. 7.

[3] W. Sombart, *The Quintessence of Capitalism*, ch. XI.

[4] R. H. Tawney, *Religion and the Rise of Capitalism*, pp. 102-132.

[5] R. H. Tawney, *op. cit.*, pp. 127-138.

[6] D. W. Howe, *The Puritan Republic of the Massachusetts Bay*, pp. 130-131; 138-139; 144. Laws against forestalling, regrating and engrossing continued until about 1820. Yale Law Journal. Vol. 36, p. 42.

[7] L. W. Bacon, *History of American Christianity*, p. 108.

[8] Howe, *op. cit.*, ch. XI; C. A. and Mary Beard, *The Rise of American Civilization*. Vol. I, pp. 52-59.

[9] T. Hamilton, *Men and Manners in America*, pp. 208-209.

[10] Francis Hall, *Travels in Canada and the United States in 1816 and 1817*, pp. 268-269.

[11] Quoted in Sombart, *op. cit.*, p. 256.

[12] Quoted in L. L. Hazard, *The Frontier in American Literature*, pp. 6-7.

[13] Quoted in W. H. Macleod, *op. cit.*, pp. 215-216.

[14] Max Weber, *Gesammelte Aufsatze zur Religionssoziologie*. Vol. I, pp. 32ff.

[15] Quoted in Phillips Russell, *Benjamin Franklin—The First Civilized American*, p. 132.

[16] A. H. Smyth, *The Writings of Benjamin Franklin*. Vol. II, p. 372.

[17] A. H. Smyth, *op. cit.* Vol. I.

[18] P. Russell, *op. cit.*, pp. 141-142.

[19] *Ibid.*

[20] V. L. Parrington, *Main Currents in American Thought*. Vol. I, pp. 88-97.

[21] Thwaites, *op. cit.* Vols. IX, X.

[22] Mississippi Valley Historical Association Proceedings. Vol. III, pp. 6off., *Quakers in the Old Northwest.*

[23] A. M. Schlesinger, *The Colonial Merchants and the American Revolution*, pp. 27ff.

[24] Weber, *op. cit.*, pp. 190-191.

[25] Mississippi Valley Historical Review. Vol. V, p. 300, *Passing of the Frontier.*

[26] Ogden, *Letters From the West, 1821-1823*, published in Thwaites, *op. cit.* Vol. XIX, pp. 92-93.

[27] Flower's *Letters*, p. 145, published in Thwaites, *op. cit.* Vol. X.

[28] Quoted in Lippincott, *op. cit.*, p. 277.

[29] Thwaites, *op. cit.* Vol. X, p. 135.

[30] Faux's *Journal* published in Thwaites, *op. cit.* Vol. X, p. 236.

[31] *Ibid.*, p. 189.

[32] Illinois State Historical Society Transactions 1905, p. 54.

[33] Pease, *op. cit.*, p. 18.

[34] Gillespie, *op. cit.*, p. 11.

[35] H. R. Schoolcraft, *Travels in the Central Portions of the Mississippi Valley*, pp. 158-159.

[36] Kofoid, *Puritan Influences*, p. 303; R. W. Patterson, *Early Society in Southern Illinois*, p. 105; J. Gillespie, *Recollections of Early Illinois and Her Noted Men*, p. 6.

[37] Wisconsin Magazine of History. Vol. VII, p. 489, *Recollections of Life in Early Wisconsin.*

[38] Minnesota History Magazine, June, 1928; Sept., 1928, *The Claim Association and Pioneer Democracy;* M. P. Shortridge, *The Transition of a Typical Frontier*, p. 32.

[39] F. C. Holliday, *op. cit.*, p. 117.

[40] George Lewis, *Impressions of America and the American Churches*, p. 326.

[41] Mississippi Valley Historical Review. Vol. IX, No. 3, *Nativism in the Forties and Fifties with Special Reference to the Mississippi Valley.*

[42] A. de Tocqueville, *Democracy in America.* Vol. I, p. 335.

[43] L. P. Powell, ed. *Historic Towns of the Western States*, p. 357.

[44] L. W. Bacon, *op. cit.*, 325ff.; American Antiquarian Society Proceedings, New Series. Vol. 29, p. 238, F. J. Turner, *Greater New England in the Middle of the Nineteenth Century.*

[45] Quoted in R. F. Vogel, *Social Life in Saint Louis*, p. 24.

[46] *Memoir of John M. Peck*, p. 88.

[47] Wisconsin Magazine of History. Vol. 7, p. 3ff., J. Schafer, *Yankee and Teuton.*

[48] A. H. Smyth, *op. cit.* Vol. II, pp. 291ff.

[49] T. Flint, *Recollections of the Last Ten Years*, pp. 233-237.

[50] J. Schafer, *op. cit.*, p. 11.

[51] Hulme's *Journal* published in Thwaites, *op. cit.* Vol. X, p. 53.

[52] *Nativism in the Forties and Fifties, etc.*, p. 194.

[53] Quoted in Kofoid, *op. cit.*, p. 319.

CHAPTER IV

NEW ECONOMIC DEVELOPMENTS AND THE ECONOMIC VIRTUES

COMMERCE and industry grew as eager business men were pushing into the West. The wealth of the country quadrupled between 1837 and 1857.[1] In the ten years following 1850, the value of industrial products increased ninety-eight per cent.[2] At the same time the number of towns was increasing rapidly. In 1840 there were but forty-four towns with a population over eight thousand. By 1860 the number had increased to one hundred and forty-one.[3]

Anxious money-seekers sprang up on all sides. The California gold strike of 1849 lured many Easterners into the West and imbued them with dreams of fabulous wealth. The fortunes from gold mining in turn set up a demand for manufactured goods.[4] During the fifties there was a tremendous rush into Iowa, Illinois, Michigan, Minnesota, Wisconsin, and Mississippi. Land speculation drew these hordes of people.[5] Kansas and Nebraska were opened to settlement in 1854 and many farmers from farther east went there in search of good farming land.

Laborers were not unaffected by the lure of wealth. A Fall River labor leader in 1846 complained, "The first lesson a boy is taught on leaving the parental roof is to get gain . . . gain wealth . . . forgetting all but self."[6]

Nor did this absorption in money-making entirely cease during and immediately following the Civil War. The high prices that resulted from the issue of the greenbacks induced many people to leave agriculture and manufacturing for more speculative ventures. Although wage earners suffered from the increased costs of living business men profited. New fortunes appeared. Speculators and army contractors, particularly, increased their fortunes tremendously.[7] The Homestead Act of 1862 opened vast areas in the West to occupation at nominal prices. With the greater immigration that followed, there was a rapid growth of land speculation accompanied by greater optimism concerning future business prospects in the West.

The older differences between the farmers and business men were not so glaring since much of the farmers' self-sufficiency had disappeared by the close of the Civil War.[8] The farmer himself was becoming a business man and producing crops for sale in the market. In some of the new Western states farmers specialized in wheat farming. They no longer produced most of the things they consumed. Productivity per worker increased with the introduction of cultivators, seed drills, reapers, mowers, and occasionally threshing machines.[9] One farm laborer in 1860 could produce more than three in 1840 and was less dependent on assistance from his neighbors on account of the greater use of farm machinery. The receipts of flour at Chicago increased tenfold and those of wheat fivefold between 1854 and 1868.[10] The farmers' concentration on pecuniary success was becoming obvious.[11]

In spite of this interest in businesslike farming, not all of the behavior traits previously emphasized by the farmers disappeared. The farmers in producing a surplus for sale thought that the profits they received were less than the profits gained by the railroads that carried their produce to market and the middlemen who passed the products on. They also felt that the prices they paid for manufactured goods were exorbitant. As a solution for this they fell back on their old virtues of neighborliness and co-operation. This was evidenced in the granger movement. They attempted to reduce the prices of farm machinery and consumers goods by buying co-operatively, and through their organizations they brought pressure to bear on the various legislatures to pass laws that would control railroads and "trusts." Along with this the grange inculcated certain virtues which had been recommended and advocated by the spokesmen for the business community. The grange was the foe of carelessness and disorder, idleness and vice, and it extolled the virtues of orderliness, industry, thrift, and economy.[12] There was still something of the idea of self-sufficiency in their emphasis on these virtues. It was not self-sufficiency in the sense that they expected to remain isolated from the rest of the world, but in the sense that they might increase the purchasing power of their income by wise economy and thrift.   They hoped that by the practice of such virtues a competence would be attained and a general condition of independence would prevail.

In commercial and industrial life a new phenomenon had appeared—the self-made man.   Not entirely new but much more conspicuous than before.   The new aspect of the self-made man was the size of the fortune he attained.   Furthermore the fortunes were being made in different lines of business.   Before the Civil War large fortunes were mainly confined to landholders and "merchant princes."[13]   After the Civil War the iron and steel industry, the oil industry, the meat-packing industry, the milling industry, the mining industry, the transportation industry, the farm-machinery industry, banking and finance, developed greatly, and as they did some individuals connected with them in one way and another came into wealth.[14]

Toward the close of the nineteenth century interested and patriotic parties enjoyed looking back to the preceding decades and enumerating the pecuniary achievements of the American business man.   Andrew Carnegie discovered so many successful people who had started at the bottom that he seemed to think this lowly start was very important for their later success.   He said many had started as mechanics and clerks.   He enumerated a long list of industrial establishments in which successful people had started as clerks or mechanics.   There were locomotive works, mechanical tool factories, saw factories, textile factories, scale factories, wagon works, the Pullman Company, car foundries, rolling mills, steel wire mills, iron foundries, carpet factories, electrical apparatus factories, seed houses, publishing houses, boiler steel factories, munition factories, sewing machine factories, agricultural implement factories, steamship companies, piano companies—in all of these the successful started as poor boys.

He found the same phenomenon in mercantile, commercial, and financial branches of business.   He said, "The millionaires who are in active control started as poor boys, and were trained in the sternest but most efficient of all schools—poverty."[15]

As the industrial and commercial development along with the greater reliance on the corporate form of enterprise increased, unforeseen possibilities of profit-making appeared. Self-help, thrift, and industry when practiced in connection with corporations produced different results from the results attained when these traits were practiced in connection with the individual enterprise. An individual's fortune and that of the business with which he was connected were no longer synonymous. Certain practices that accompanied the management of corporations were thought at variance with the accepted and approved type of business conduct. It was feared by some that business expansion and the heavy credit obligations incurred by corporations would be economically disastrous.[16] Others hoped to limit the corporations by passing laws against their organization.[17]

Immediately following the Civil War, in fact even shortly before the Civil War, economic conduct overflowed the traditional boundaries. This was so obvious that historians have considered the period one of unbridled license, a period in which morals in business and public life had reached a very low ebb.[18] The successful business men of the period have been called buccaneers. There is the story of Commodore Vanderbilt's attempt to buy out the Erie Railroad. He obtained an injunction against the issue of any more securities by the management—that is, Jay Gould, Jim Fiske, and Daniel Drew. They ignored the injunction, put the printing presses to work and unloaded worthless stock on Vanderbilt. Then when faced with possible arrest for contempt, they took the books of the Erie and moved their office to New Jersey where the New York law could not be enforced. Here they maintained an armed encampment against a possible attack by Vanderbilt's forces.[19] In many cases business became armed warfare between hired followers of different individuals trying to get control or maintain control of various properties.

No new economic virtues were developed for this more complicated economic life. Reliance was placed on the advocacy of self-help, thrift, industry, and honesty. The Puritan teachings were still influential. The Puritans established the principles that were generally followed in public education. The religious purpose in instruction dominated almost all the schools in America.[20] The lessons taught emphasized industry, humility, and self-control. Such manuals as McGuffey's Eclectic Readers, some seventy or eighty million of which have been used by American school children, were means by which instruction was given. Moral homilies were preached on such subjects as "The Sin of Vanity," "The Mockeries of the Fooleries of Life," "Never Give Up," "Self-Reliance," "Look Before You Leap," "Advantages of Industry," "The Importance of Well-Spent Youth," "Procrastination." In inculcating morals in the young the animal kingdom was used for illustrations of the economic virtues. For example, an idle boy asked a dog to play with him but the dog replied, "No, I must not be idle; I must catch a hare for my master's dinner." After attempting to mislead a bird and a horse into idleness and not succeeding in doing so the little boy concludes, "What! is nobody idle? Then little boys must not be idle." Frugality of dress was still emphasized. The peacock was described in the Reader. It is "haughty and proud and loves to display its fine colors." Consequently the moral to be drawn was, "Little boys and girls, be not like the peacock, proud and vain, on account of your beauty and fine clothes, for humility and goodness are always to be preferred to beauty."[21]

Industry, self-help, and punctuality were much emphasized. In McGuffey's Fifth Reader a reading lesson starts:

> Work, work, my boy, be not afraid;
>   Look labor boldly in the face;
> Take up the hammer or the spade,
>   And blush not for your humble place.

Another exercise starts by asserting, "Rely upon it that the ancients were right; both in morals and intellect we give the final shape to our characters by our own efforts." The selection, which is taken from the oratorical efforts of a politician, goes on to prove that native talents are useless without hard work; in fact, too much native endowment is a handicap since it tempts one to shirk and lie down on the job, and then one is easily surpassed by the duller but the more industrious. The conclusion of the oration is, There can be "No Excellence Without Labor."

Punctuality was taught by showing the awful effects of being "behind time." An engineer wrecks his train and kills fifty passengers because he is behind his schedule; an innocent man is hanged because the messenger who is bringing the governor's pardon arrives too late. His watch was slow. A business house fails because a messenger is too slow in delivering the funds that would have established the firm's credit. The selection ends: "The best-laid plans, the most important affairs, the fortunes of individuals, the weal of nations, honor, happiness, life itself, are daily sacrificed, because somebody is 'behind time'."[22]

In this manner the schools gave the traditional virtues continued life and wide circulation. No definite codes of conduct were developed for all the intricate situations and problems that arose in economic activity. Industry, thrift, honesty, etc., were marks of virtue, but the meaning of these words was vague and indefinite, nor were there always satisfactory means by which the presence of these virtues could be detected.

Very frequently pecuniary success was taken as a test for virtue. This was in line with previous pronouncements, such as those of Benjamin Franklin.[23] Few thought that economic conditions had changed. Books were written to show that virtue was not without its reward. One of these books was rather extravagantly entitled: *"Kings of Fortune; or, the Triumphs and Achievements of Noble, Self-Made Men, whose brilliant careers have honored their calling, blessed humanity, and whose lives furnish instruction for the young, entertainment for the old, and valuable lessons for the aspirants of fortune,"* by W. R. Houghton, A.M., N. Y., 1885. Some of the more prosaic titles were: *Poor Boys Who Became Famous, Millionaires and Kings of Enterprise, Men Who Have Risen, Captains of Industry.* These books, as well as the millionaires themselves, used the traditional economic virtues to show how they were at the bottom of most of the great fortunes that were accumulated. Spokesmen for the successful were anxious also to indicate the social benefits of these large fortunes. They argued that large fortunes increased the productivity of the country, more people were employed in the works financed by the millionaire, more wages were distributed, and greater purchasing power enabled the population at large to consume a greater variety of commodities. The virtues came in as the means by which all this was made possible.

Let us see if these wealthy people became more explicit concerning the actual meaning of economic virtues; see if their behavior was at all connected with the virtues; and if these virtues had any other importance for economic life. Not all the fortunes will be analyzed, but attention will be confined to those individuals who made their fortunes from the steel and oil industries.

Andrew Carnegie was, for a time, somewhat of a spokesman for the successful and gave voice to certain traits of behavior which were understood by him and other business men as the proper economic virtues. The virtues enabled one to accumulate wealth and by so doing increase the economic welfare of the entire society. These virtues were not always clearly or consistently expressed, but they give some indication of the feelings of Carnegie and other business men on the subject.

Carnegie enumerated the basic principles involved in acquiring great fortune in a talk to young men which he called, "The Road to Business Success." First, one should start at the bottom. "It is well that young men should begin at the beginning and occupy the most subordinate positions. Many of the leading business men of Pittsburgh had a serious responsibility thrust upon them at the very threshold of their career. They were introduced to the broom, and spent the first hours of their business lives sweeping out the office." After starting at the beginning one should aim high. "Say to yourself, 'My place is at the top.' Be king in your dreams." Life must be reduced to a matter of calculation. Control behavior with an eye to its effect on income. Drunkenness must be avoided, so must speculation. Too much speculation may ruin one's credit standing. "Nothing kills credit sooner in any Bank Board than the knowledge that either firms or men engage in speculation. . . . The moment a man is known to speculate, his credit is impaired, and soon there-after it is gone."

Don't be too reckless in assisting others. This is not lack of virtue. One must think of the greater virtue, not the lesser.

The third and last danger against which I shall warn you . . . is the perilous habit of endorsing—all the more danger-ous, inasmuch as it assails one generally in the garb of friend-ship. . . . If you owe anything, all your capital and all your effects are a solemn trust in your hands to be held inviolable for the security of those who have trusted you. Nothing can be done by you with honor which jeopardizes these first claims upon you. When a man in debt endorses for another, it is not his own credit or his own capital he risks, it is that of his creditors. He vio-lates a trust.

There are not only acts which the aspirant to fortune must shun, there are certain things which he must conspicuously do.

There is one sure mark of the coming partner, the future millionaire; his revenues always exceed his expenditures. He begins to save yearly, almost as soon as he begins to earn. No matter how little it may be possible to save, save that little. . . . The little you have saved will prove the basis for an amount of credit utterly surprising to you. Capitalists trust the saving man. . . . It is not capital that your seniors require, it is the man who has proved he has the business habits which create capi-tal, and to create it in the best of all possible ways, as far as self-discipline is concerned, is by adjusting his habits to his means. Gentlemen, it is the first hundred dollars saved which tells. Begin at once to lay up something. The bee predominates in the future millionaire.

Of course one must not hide his light under a bushel. One's virtue must be seen if it is to be rewarded. "The rising man must do something exceptional, and beyond the range of his special department. He must attract attention."

Then finally:

Here is the prime condition of success, the great secret: concentrate your energy, thought, and capital exclusively upon the business in which you are engaged. Having begun in one line, resolve to fight it out on that line, to lead in it; adopt every improvement, have the best machinery, and know the most about it.[24]

These traits which Carnegie thinks essential for success are practically a restatement of the economic virtues which had developed out of the activities of the earlier business groups in the West mixed with doses of Puritanism and applied to different economic conditions. But it is a secularized Puritanism; one is not being thrifty merely for the sake of righteousness but because thrift is admired by men of means and they may be willing to recognize and assist one who has the reputation of being thrifty. Speculation is not merely dangerous on its own account, it may damage one's credit standing. Independence becomes a matter of refraining from entangling financial alliances which may suddenly bring about loss of funds. One's relations to one's fellows are, to a degree, determined by pecuniary considerations. And one's personal conduct should be regulated in the light of how the income is affected by the conduct.

But the use of these traits as means to fortune does not necessarily make the traits into economic virtues. Carnegie goes on to show how these traits and the possession of great wealth work toward the economic welfare of society as a whole. Accumulation of money means investment in industries that improve economic welfare. This accumulation is called thrift. "We could not have had anything more than the savage had, except for thrift. . . . There was nothing built, no great progress made as long as men remained thriftless savages."

Furthermore, "as a rule, you will find that the saving man is a temperate man, a good husband and father, a peaceful, law-abiding citizen."[25]

Carnegie feels that wealth does not always come from "savings in the ordinary sense of the word." But great fortunes should be encouraged because they can be devoted to the welfare of society. "A man's first duty is to make a competence and be independent," that is, have a considerable fortune.

But his whole duty does not end there. It is his duty to do something for his needy neighbors who are less favored than himself. It is his duty to contribute to the general good of the community in which he lives. . . . To try to make the world in some way better than you found it, is to have a noble motive in life. Your surplus wealth should contribute to the development of your own character and place you in the rank of nature's noblemen.

Carnegie was speaking for the "New Wealth." But what was the relationship between the economic virtues he advocated and the behavior of the successful money-makers? The careers of the millionaires connected with the oil industry will be considered first and then some of those connected with the iron and steel industry will be investigated.

FOOTNOTES FOR CHAPTER IV

[1] K. Coman, *Industrial History of the United States*, p. 232.

[2] W. F. Gephart, *Transportation and Industrial Development in the Middle West*, p. 248.

[3] K. Coman, *op. cit.*, p. 233.

[4] A. C. Cole, *The Era of the Civil War*, pp. 9, 10.

[5] Mississippi Valley Historical Society Proceedings. Vol. III, pp. 212ff., D. E. Clark, *Westward Movement in the Upper Mississippi Valley During the Fifties*.

[6] N. J. Ware, *The Industrial Worker, 1840-1860*, p. 24 and ch. 3 on *The Spirit of the Age*.

[7] On these conditions see W. C. Mitchell, *A History of the Greenbacks*, 1903, pp. 347, 395, 397, 399.

[8] S. J. Buck, *The Granger Movement*, p. 238.

[9] A. C. Cole, *op. cit.*, pp. 10, 49, 80.

[10] A. Nevins, *op. cit.*, p. 160.

[11] J. Reynolds, *My Own Times*, p. 248; G. Lewis, *Impressions of America and the American Churches*, p. 327.

[12] S. J. Buck, *op. cit.*, p. 299.

[13] B. J. Hendrick, *The Age of Big Business*, ch. 1.

[14] A. Nevins, *op, cit.*, ch. 2.

[15] Andrew Carnegie, writing in the New York Tribune, April 13, 1890, reprinted in A. Carnegie, *The Empire of Business*, pp. 106-109.

[16] The Living Age. Vol. XV, 1847, *Trading Morals*.

[17] C. R. Fish, *The Rise of the Common Man*, pp. 54-56.

[18] J. F. Rhodes asserted that by 1854 "Mammon had become the national saint." *History of the United States*. Vol. III, p. 80; E. P. Oberholtzer said, "Wealth had become such a mighty goal (after the Civil War) that no one questioned the means by which it had been acquired." E. P. Oberholtzer, *History of the United States Since the Civil War*, Vol. II, pp. 538-614; on the other hand, A. Nevins believed this "orgy and corruption" was confined to a few and that the country as a whole met fairly rigid moral standards. A. Nevins, *op. cit.*, p. 214.

[19] For the exciting performances of the contenders for the control of the Erie railroad see, *High Finance in the Sixties*, edited by Frederick C. Hicks.

[20] E. P. Cubberly, *Public Education in the United States*, pp. 28, 29.

[21] Quoted in Mark Sullivan, *Our Times.* Vol. II, pp. 20, 30-33, 135, 136.

[22] McGuffey's Fifth Eclectic Reader, 1879, pp. 162, 231.

[23] Franklin, however, might have been frightened by the great developments of industrialism.   He was opposed to industrialism.

[24] A. Carnegie, *The Empire of Business*, pp. 3-10.

[25] *Ibid.*, pp. 95-99.

CHAPTER V

THE SELF-MADE MAN IN THE OIL INDUSTRY

THE oil industry was highly speculative.[1] After the first well was drilled in western Pennsylvania in 1859 there was a tremendous rush to the oil fields; wells were sunk as fast as possible. No one knew beforehand in just what spot oil would be discovered. Some individuals made a fortune overnight while others with the same industry and the same care in choosing what seemed to be a promising locality got nothing. The shrewder individuals waited until an oil well had been tapped and then acquired adjacent land, drilled a well and attempted to tap their neighbor's well.[2]

These early efforts at oil-producing exemplified the enterprise and gambling spirit of that section of the population which had turned its attention to money-making. After some had made fortunes in the enterprise, others strove to emulate them. The rules of the game were few: Each individual looked after himself; he tried to get his oil flowing before the supply gave out and before others had tapped the same oil pocket. Sometimes success was insured by wrecking the derrick and machinery of a competitor. The only difficulty with this competitive struggle was that it was mutually ruinous. If all the drillers succeeded in sinking productive wells the large amount of oil "produced" would flood the market and no one would make any money. This difficulty was reflected in the great fluctuations in crude oil prices. In January, 1860, oil was twenty dollars a barrel, but so much was drilled in the succeeding months that by the end of 1861 the price had fallen to ten cents a barrel. For the first fifteen years or so of the industry's existence oil prices fluctuated so rapidly no one could determine how long he would retain his fortune or even whether he had one at all.

The producers had other troubles besides those of unregulated production. There was at first no large purchaser or organized market to which they might send their oil. Furthermore shipping facilities were inadequate. Teamsters hauled the oil from the wells to barges. The barges loaded with barrels of oil were then towed to Pittsburgh via the Allegheny River. The teamsters had a monopoly on their part of the transportation. The producer paid the rates that were demanded or else his oil was not hauled to the barges. The teamsters thrived as a result of this strategic position in which they found themselves. When they saw their monopoly slipping as pipe lines were introduced, they turned out in full force to tear up the pipes, burn the storage tanks, and try to force the producers to return to the earlier mode of transportation. Although they were unsuccessful, their earlier labor was not in vain. Some of them retired with an adequate competence.

Barge transportation was also short-lived. Here the railroad destroyed the business. But before barge transportation disappeared a few were able to gain a fortune and get into the oil industry. J. J. Vandergrift, for example, got his start in this business. He had started in the shipping industry on the Mississippi River, and, of course, started as a poor boy. He began as a cabin boy and finally became commander and owner of his own steamers. The Civil War put an end to this business, so he moved to Pittsburgh. He heard about the great demand for barrels in the oil regions, so he towed four thousand up the Allegheny, had them filled with oil, and returned to sell his cargo. He saw a bulk-boat someone was using and decided it would be an improvement over the older smaller barges. He ordered a dozen of the bulk-boats, had them filled with oil, and towed them to Pittsburgh. The profits were large. On one trip alone he made $70,000.[3] Vandergrift invested in pipe lines as they became practicable, went into oil-producing, and eventually was taken into the Standard Oil group.

Conflicts between the oil-producers and the shippers were not the only conflicts the industry experienced. The producers, the refiners, the railroad shippers, the pipe-line shippers were all struggling with one another and all attempting to wriggle into a position where they would be able to dictate conditions and terms to the other groups. The only difficulty that stood in the way was the individualistic animus. The producers would organize only to discover that they could not control their own members. The ultimate dominance of the Standard group was in part due to the fact that they were able to maintain a collusive control over refining by a well-organized combination.

It is sometimes suggested that the Rockefeller group was the only one attempting to gain monopoly power. This aim dominated all of the groups. The activities of the teamsters has already been mentioned. The same thing was attempted by the pipe-line owners. The Empire Transportation Company, a pipe line controlled by the Pennsylvania Railroad and connecting with the Philadelphia and Erie, attempted to control the transportation of oil. But the ten lines that connected with the Philadelphia and Erie could not come to satisfactory agreements over rates. They were afraid of each other, and each road continued making its own rates even after they agreed to stabilize the rates. The producers had attempted to organize, restrict production, and maintain prices at a satisfactory level. The Petroleum Producers Agency and the Producers Union were organizations that attempted to monopolize production and present a united front against the refiners and the shippers. Nor were their means of keeping the organizations together either mild or gentle. Ida Tarbell says:

There was nothing but public opinion to hold the producers to their pledge. But public opinion in those days in the oil regions was fearless and active and asserted itself in the daily newspapers and in every meeting of the association. The whole body of oil men became a vigilance committee intent on keeping one another loyal to the pledge. Men who appeared at church on Sunday in silk hats, carrying gold-headed canes—there were such in the oil regions in 1872—now stole out at night to remote localities to hunt down rumors of drilling wells. If they found them true, their dignity did not prevent their cutting the tools loose or carrying off a band wheel.[4]

The same tactics and ambitions seemed to characterize other participants in the oil industry as well as Rockefeller and his associates.

As for the individuals who were successful in the oil industry, the best known is John D. Rockefeller himself. He was born on a farm in central New York in 1839. His family, like others of their time, moved West and settled near Cleveland, Ohio. Rockefeller was early instructed in the traditional economic virtues and seemed to think that frugality, thrift, and industry were quite important traits of character to possess. One should also possess a calculating habit of mind by which one could be thrifty and industrious most profitably.

One of the bits of advice he later gave to aspirants to fortune grew out of his early experience.

Among the early experiences that were helpful to me that I recollect with pleasure was one in working a few days for a neighbor in digging potatoes—a very enterprising, thrifty farmer who could dig a great many potatoes. I was a boy of perhaps thirteen or fourteen years of age, and it kept me very busy from morning until night. It was a ten-hour day. And as I was saving these little sums I soon learned that I could get as much interest for fifty dollars loaned at seven per cent—the legal rate in the state of New York at that time for a year—as I could earn by digging potatoes for one hundred days. The impression was gaining ground with me that it was a good thing to let the money be my slave and not make myself a slave to money.[5]

The value of thrift and industry is to be judged by its effect on net profit.

The enterprising youth went to Cleveland at the age of sixteen to amass his fortune. After some difficulty he obtained a job for which he was to receive fifty dollars for three months' work. He stayed with the firm until he had a position as bookkeeper at $500 a year. He was offered $700, but he decided he was worth at least $800, so he left to seek more profitable ventures.[6]

He met M. B. Clark, who had $2,000, and wanted to go into business for himself if he could find someone with a little capital to contribute. Clark was another enterprising individual with habits of thrift and industry. He had left England at the age of twenty to seek his fortune in America. He arrived penniless in Boston in 1847 and eventually gravitated to Ohio. He worked at odd jobs, wood chopper, teamster, and a sort of man-of-all-work. He saved his money.[7]

The major part of Rockefeller's contribution to the business was obtained from his father. He says he put up about $700, and his father gave him $1,000.[8] With this capital he joined Clark and they started a produce house. Rockefeller borrowed some money from his father and some $2,000 from a bank for the expansion of the business. Patriotism did not lure Rockefeller and Clark into the army during the Civil War, but the war contributed to their profits. The business of furnishing army supplies was lucrative. The partners were even ready to expand into new ventures.

In 1862 Samuel Andrews asked them to back him in an oil refinery. The oil industry had demonstrated that wealth was to be found therein, and refining was less risky than oil-producing. The partners contributed $4,000. The refinery prospered, perhaps due to Andrews's proficiency in perfecting the refining process. Clark and Rockefeller contributed more funds and had $100,000 in the refinery. Rockefeller was encouraged, so he sold his interest in the produce house and went into the oil firm, which was thereafter called Rockefeller and Andrews.

In this company Rockefeller attended to the business side of things while Andrews managed the manufacturing process. Rockefeller applied to the business the same frugality that characterized his personal life. Everything was to be saved and utilized and the business was to be as independent as possible. The company made its own barrels and eliminated middlemen by buying direct from the oil-producers. Rockefeller was quite the serious, sober, and secretive young business man. Moments of joy enlivened his life occasionally, especially when he had driven a particularly close bargain. One of his acquaintances said:

> The only time I ever saw John Rockefeller enthusiastic was when a report came in from the creek that his buyer had secured a cargo of oil at a figure much below the market price. He bounded from his chair with a shout of joy, danced up and down, hugged me, threw up his hat, acted so like a madman that I have never forgotten it.[9]

Business thrived. A new firm was organized with William Rockefeller. It was called William Rockefeller and Company, and through it another refinery was constructed. A third concern was organized to be called Rockefeller and Company, which was to be a selling agency with headquarters in New York city. In 1867 these three firms combined with S. V. Harkness and H. M. Flagler into a new firm called Rockefeller, Andrews, and Flagler. The former partnerships had brought in new capital and had obtained more properties connected with the oil business.

In 1870 The Standard Oil Company of Ohio was organized and took over the properties of the former partnership. It was capitalized at $1,000,000. Those interested in it were J. D. and William A. Rockefeller, Samuel Andrews, Henry M. Flagler, and Stephen V. Harkness. William Rockefeller was quite different from his brother. He was not so frugal in his habits nor so pious. Although his brother did not fully approve of William's ways he did not object to his presence because William was popular with the oil-producers and could purchase oil at low prices.[10] Harkness was a Cleveland merchant with strong financial connections. Flagler had gone into partnership with Clark when Rockefeller left and finally bought Clark out. He seemed to have many of the traits of John D. Rockefeller.

In the first ten years or so of the corporation's existence its controllers seemed to have been very successful in ridding themselves of competitors. This feat and the extension of the corporation's power was largely due, according to the Commissioner of Corporations, to railroad rebates.[11] The new company was following the recognized procedure in the oil industry of gaining some advantage that would lift it out of the realm of competition.

The railroads were competing vigorously for traffic, and the company at Cleveland was in a position to play off the trunk lines against one another. If the roads established "a community of interest" shipping by water via the Great Lakes could be resorted to. The only problem for the Standard was to prevent the growth of other large refineries, since in that case the railroads might play off one refinery against another.

The Standard group first attempted to control rates through an organization known as the South Improvement Company.[12] This concern was to bargain with the roads and guarantee them enough oil so that it would be profitable for them to give the refiners large rebates. The rebates on refined oil were about 25 to 40 per cent of the gross rates. As long as the South Improvement Company was able to get such advantages for its members those outside the organization were in a fair way to be ruined. About twenty of the twenty-five independent refiners in Cleveland sold out to the Standard Oil Company. The arrangement aroused antagonism among the surviving independents, and they succeeded in April, 1872, in getting the Pennsylvania legislature to revoke the charter of the South Improvement Company.

However, the Standard continued to get rebates on its shipments of oil. It also continued the process of buying in desirable independents. Warden Frew and Company of Philadelphia, Charles Lockhart of Pittsburgh, and Charles Pratt and Company of New York were acquired in 1874. Under a device similar to the South Improvement Company other independents were either ruined or acquired. The Central Association of Refiners was an organization in which the Standard Oil Company was to arrange rates for the refiners with the railroads, buy and sell oil, and determine the quantity of output.

This task of controlling refiners and transportation rates was not accomplished without considerable opposition. Not only did the Standard Oil have to control the railroads, it also had to prevent the independents from using the pipelines as a means of fighting the Standard.

Here, again, success depended on which group was able to maintain collective action. The pipe lines had been started by the independents as early as 1865. After they had been proved practicable the Standard group entered the field. In 1874 they attained control of the United Pipe Lines, which was doing some 30 per cent of the pipe-line business in the oil regions of Pennsylvania. Agreements were made with the Erie and the New York Central regarding rates and the apportionment of traffic. When this move was made the other pipe lines allied themselves with railroads. The Empire Transportation Company, one of the largest, joined with the Pennsylvania Railroad in a fight against the Standard. It even built refineries and threatened to invade what had been the private preserve of the Standard group. This move started a rate war between the railroads, during which rates were cut below cost. The Pennsylvania succumbed first and sold the Empire Transportation Company to the Standard Oil Company. Then the Standard acquired the Columbia Conduit Company, which gave it control of all the important pipe-line systems.

This did not end the struggle. The independents proposed building a pipe line from the Pennsylvania oil region to the sea-coast. The project succeeded, and the Tide Water Pipe Company was able to pipe oil directly into New York City. The Standard then started to construct through pipe lines to points in New Jersey and also to acquire independent refineries in and about New York City which would prevent the Tide Water Company from marketing its oil. The Tide Water was not only fighting the Standard Oil Company, it had the railroads allied against it, since they would be ruined if the pipe lines made themselves entirely independent of the railroads. The Tide Water Company finally surrendered and entered into an agreement with the Standard Oil Company which practically made it a member of the Standard group.

After an effective control over the refining business had been attained the Standard Oil Company was organized as a trust. The trust agreement was declared illegal by the Ohio courts in 1892. In 1899 the Standard group reorganized as a holding company in the state of New Jersey. This concern exchanged its stock for the stock which had been previously controlled by the trustees. The trustees in the earlier organization were made directors in the new holding company. The result was that the monopoly position of the Standard was virtually unchanged.

According to the Commissioner of Corporations the Standard Oil Company averaged something over 24 per cent per year in dividends. The report goes on to state that the source of the power which made possible these high dividends was in such practices as the use of rebates, espionage on competitors' business, operation of bogus independents, and local price cutting.[13]

Whatever may have been the reasons for their success the leaders in the industry gave plausibility to Carnegie's Road to

Business Success since their careers followed his pattern in many respects.

It has been mentioned that J. J. Vandergrift, John D. Rockefeller, William Rockefeller, and M. B. Clark started as poor boys and "worked up." Charles Pratt started as a farm laborer, gravitated to the city, and at the age of twenty started as a clerk in a paint and oil shop in New York City. H. M. Flagler was the son of a missionary preacher and at the age of fourteen set out for Ohio in search of his fortune. H. H. Rogers came from a poor family in New England and started as an ambitious salesman for Charles Pratt and Company in New York. J. D. Archbold, a Methodist minister's son, started work in a country store in western Pennsylvania which happened to be located in the very region in which oil was struck.

The oil millionaires were thrifty not so much in the sense that they attempted to husband their revenue in a way that would insure them a competence, but in the sense that they reduced their economic affairs to a "rational" plan whereby they attempted to discover in what direction thrift would bring the greatest net return. Thrift per se was not useful unless it increased the opportunities for increasing one's income.

The dictum that "one should not allow one's expenditures to exceed one's income" seemed to apply to personal expenditures for consumption purposes. This was recommended as much for the good effect it would have on bankers and prospective business associates as anything else. It was to indicate one's serious purpose in life and to show others that one was to be trusted. There was no prejudice against indebtedness for business purposes; that is, loans which were to be invested in business instead of in personal expenditures. Few of the individuals would have got along if they had not borrowed money. Rockefeller tells us that he was able to enter the produce house with Clark because his father loaned him $1,000. The father would not advance the money until he was assured of his son's thrift and industry. Flagler was able to go into partnership with Rockefeller and others because S. V. Harkness backed him for $100,000. Before this Flagler lost $40,000 in salt manufacture in Michigan, but he had known Rockefeller when Rockefeller was in the produce business and was thought an enterprising individual. J. D. Archbold worked in a store owned by W. H. Abbott. Abbott had made some fortunate speculations in oil production and assisted his young clerk in starting out as an oil broker.

Industriousness consisted of devout attention to money-making by whatever means were necessary. This was considered of great value to one's moral nature. Charles Pratt announced, "There is nothing under God's heaven so important to the individual as to acquire the power to earn his own living; to be able to stand alone if necessary; to be dependent upon no one; to be indispensable to some one."[14] And Rockefeller was convinced that "the only thing which is of lasting benefit to a man is that which he does for himself. Money which comes to him without effort on his part is seldom a benefit and often a curse."[15] This individual effort is to be taken in a pecuniary sense. It doesn't mean that by manual effort one accumulates and saves his earnings until he finally acquires a competence and enters a state of independence. Money may be acquired from relatives or a bank, but this is supposed to represent individual effort; it is effort in establishing one's credit position. The only type of fortune which these men interpreted as not coming from personal effort was that which was completely inherited from one's family. Fortunes coming from monopoly position were interpreted as being the result of individual effort since it required some effort to acquire the monopoly.

These men were also endowed with religious purpose. To Rockefeller money-making was a religious duty. He said, "I believe it is a religious duty to get all the money you can fairly and honestly, to keep all you can, and to give away all you can."[16] Religion was considered a great aid to the development of industry, perseverance, and ultimate success. John D. Rockefeller devoted his spare time to teaching a Bible class. Although William Rockefeller lacked the great piety of his brother, he was pleased to lease a $25,000 parsonage in Tarrytown to the Baptist preacher for one dollar a year. When Flagler became interested in developing Florida, one of his first demands was that a church be established. He further insisted that "Sunday is to be kept at Palm Beach. Its observance is one of the features of the place." At least so Flagler's minister in Florida reports.[17]

Another quality these men highly regarded was prudence. It seemed proper to let others take the risks connected with new discoveries or the introduction of new techniques. The innovators were not always the successful. In the oil industry the Standard Oil group did not make the first discoveries of oil, did not discover inventions necessary for oil-production, did not discover or invent new means of transportation such as the pipe line, and did not make the first improvements in the refining process.[18]

From the pecuniary point of view this was sound policy. Carnegie is reported to have said, "Pioneering don't pay." One who attempted to pioneer in the oil industry was inclined to agree with Carnegie. First, this pioneer started some pipe lines which were successful. He said:

Then the teamsters threatened to kill any one who worked on the pipe line or who used it. They would drive astraddle of it, dig down to it, put logging chains around it and drag it out of the ground, and leave the oil, worth $4 to $5 a barrel, running to waste out of the holes. I sent to New York for some carbines, hired twenty-five men to patrol the line, and put a stop to that. I put up the line as security for some debts owed by my partner, under an agreement that when its profits had paid the debt it was to be returned to me. The debt was wiped out in a few months, but I never got the line back. . . . I had no money left to sue for it. That was the end of my pipe line. . . . Then I went to refining oil and, with a partner, built one of the first big refineries in the oil regions. There has been no oil refined in this country since 1870 without the help of my improvements. Some I patented, some I did not. . . . We made $12,500 in fifteen months although we paid as high as $8 a barrel for crude. I worked like a slave to make good the loss of $100,000 in my pipe line. I worked and watched day and night, and knew I was beating them all making oil. My partners were church elders, who could never find words enough to express their indignation about the way my pipe line had been taken from me, and so virtuous that they never smoked a cigar or drank a drop. I got into no end of lawsuits with them, and I lost my property again. I sold a part interest in my patent to some one who was afterward taken into this oil combination, and it now claims that they own all my patents. They have frightened off or bought off every one who has tried to use any of my inventions.[19]

Management of technical processes was no sure avenue to wealth.

FOOTNOTES FOR CHAPTER V

[1] *The Commercial and Financial Chronicle*, Oct. 21, 1865, p. 515.

[2] These competitive conditions are described by one of the contestants in *Derricks of Destiny, The Autobiography of Samuel Gamble Payne.*

[3] Ida Tarbell, *The History of the Standard Oil Company.* Vol. I, p. 16.

[4] *Ibid.* Vol. I, p. 115. Miss Tarbell feels that the producers resorted to such tactics under pressure from the refiners. The producers really wanted a free field for all contestants, but when the refiners combined into a monopoly against them, the only defense was in combination. This may have been true, but it would not explain the monopoly enjoyed by the teamsters nor the arrangements regarding rates which the railroads attempted to observe.

[5] *Ibid.* Vol. I, p. 42.

[6] J. D. Rockefeller, *Random Reminiscences of Men and Events*, pp. 36-40.

[7] I. Tarbell, *op. cit.* Vol. I, p. 42.

[8] J. D. Rockefeller, *op. cit.*, p. 41.

[9] Quoted in Tarbell, *op. cit.* Vol. I, p. 43.

[10] Tarbell, *op. cit.* Vol. I, p. 50.

[11] *Report on the Petroleum Industry*, 1907, Part I, p. 22; G. H. Montague in *The Rise and Progress of the Standard Oil Company* is inclined to attribute the rapid rise of the Standard to the ability and foresight of its managers.

[12] *Report on the Petroleum Industry*, Part I, pp. 22ff.

[13] *Ibid.* Part II, pp. 40, 666.

[14] Quoted in Sherman Williams, *Some Successful Americans*, p. 134.

[15] J. D. Rockefeller, *op. cit.*, p. 152.

[16] McClure's Magazine. Vol. 25, p. 393, 1905, Ida Tarbell, The Character of John D. Rockefeller.

[17] H. M. Flagler—1830-1913, In Memoriam, in the New York Public Library.

[18] H. D. Lloyd, *Wealth Against Commonwealth*, pp. 462-464.

[19] Quoted in H. D. Lloyd, *op. cit.*, pp. 186-187.

CHAPTER VI

THE SELF-MADE MAN IN
THE IRON AND STEEL INDUSTRY

CARNEGIE, in his Autobiography, has familiarized the public with certain details of his career. He arrived in this country in 1848 at the age of thirteen. His first work was as a bobbin boy in a cotton factory at $1.20 a week. He was recommended by his Uncle Hogan to David Brooks, manager of a telegraph office, and the latter employed Andrew as a messenger.[1] Carnegie learned telegraphy, impressed the manager of the office, and when an operator was needed at Greensburg (thirty miles from Pittsburgh) was appointed to fill the vacancy. This was a temporary position. When Carnegie returned to Pittsburgh he became acquainted with Thomas A. Scott, at that time superintendent of the Pittsburgh division of the Pennsylvania Railroad. They met when Scott came into the office to send telegrams. When Scott needed a clerk and telegraph operator on the railroad he offered the job to Carnegie at a salary of thirty-five dollars a month.[2]

In this position Carnegie had opportunity "to attract the attention of those over him." In Scott's absence a serious wreck had tied up the trains on the entire division. Carnegie proceeded to telegraph orders to clear up the wreckage and start the trains moving. He signed Scott's name to the dispatches.[3] This impressed his superior officers, and perhaps he was not far wrong, at least regarding his own future, when he said, "The battle of life is already half won by the young man who is brought personally in contact with high officials."[4] As his personal contact with the officials continued Scott recommended various investments to him. The first was ten shares of Adams Express stock. Carnegie didn't have the necessary $500, so he borrowed it from his uncle. The Carnegie home was mortgaged as security for the loan.[5] Another deal was with T. T. Woodruff, who had some patents for the manufacture of a sleeping car. Scott agreed to place two of the cars on the Pennsylvania Railroad and Carnegie took an eighth interest in the venture. This cost $217.50, which he succeeded in borrowing from a local banker.[6] He says he made his first considerable sum from this source.

Carnegie mentions no other investments, but an historian of the Carnegie Steel Company says that Carnegie, with the aid of his chief, Mr. Scott, engaged in a number of enterprises. He even seemed to be something of a speculator.

> Besides the Woodruff Sleeping Car Company and the Columbia Oil Company, in both of which Mr. Scott gave him an interest, . . . he had interests in a scheme for building telegraph lines along the Pennsylvania Railroad, in a construction company, in a project for establishing a sutler's business in soldiers' camps, in a horse-trading concern, in a bridge-building company, in a locomotive works, in the Duck Creek Oil Company, in the Birmingham Passenger (horse-car) Railroad, in the Third National Bank, in the Pittsburgh Grain Elevator, in the Citizen's Passenger Railroad, and the Dutton Oil Company.[7]

Not only did this seem to reveal a tendency toward speculation, but it was rather a large list of interests for one who recommended attention to a single enterprise.

As for "self-help" to this point in his career, Carnegie was indebted to his uncle for his initial start as a telegraph operator. He gained employment with Scott of the Pennsylvania Railroad because Scott saw him in the office (Carnegie was the only clerk when Scott came in), and then remembered him when he needed an operator. Carnegie further impressed his presence on Scott at the time of the railroad wreck. Scott then recommended various investments. Money from his uncle and a mortgage on the house owned by Carnegie's mother made the initial investment possible. This gave him enough credit standing to raise a loan from a local banker and invest in the Sleeping Car Company. Further investments were possible. The business knowledge and financial affiliations of Mr. Scott were of great value to Carnegie in many of the investments.

Carnegie's first venture in the iron business was with T. N.

Miller, Henry Phipps, and Andrew Kloman. The four of them formed a partnership and started a small iron mill.[8] Kloman was a mechanic with an established reputation for making very excellent axles. Miller was a purchasing agent for the Pittsburgh, Fort Wayne and Chicago Railroad. Phipps's history had been something like Carnegie's, at least so Carnegie says. He is reputed to have spent his first quarter on an advertisement in the "Pittsburgh Dispatch," "A willing boy wishes work." He obtained a position as errand boy with the firm of Dillworth and Bidwell, "and as was then the custom, his first duty every morning was to sweep the office. . . . There was no holding back a boy like that. It was the old story."[9] He met Mr. Miller, who loaned him enough to go into the iron-mill partnership.[10]

The business was quite profitable. This seemed due to two circumstances: the Civil War and the firm's railroad connections. The Civil War brought the price of axles from two cents a pound to twelve cents. Profits were insured if orders could be attained. This difficulty was not insuperable since Miller gave the company the Fort Wayne business and recommended the company to other railroads.[11] It seems that Carnegie's chief asset in the Kloman crowd was his friendship with railroad officials. He got contracts.[12]

Conflicts and disagreements developed. Kloman and Phipps forced Miller out of the business.[13] Miller's capital was put into the hands of T. M. Carnegie (Andrew's brother) as trustee. Carnegie sided with Miller and they built the Cyclops Mill in 1864. The competition was not pleasing. Although Kloman and Phipps were not anxious to join forces with the Cyclops Mills, T. M. Carnegie persuaded them to do so. The two competing mills were united and called the Union Iron Mills. Miller refused to reunite because he thought the business would not be profitable, so he sold out to Carnegie, thus closing his opening into millionairedom and incidentally giving Carnegie about 39 per cent of the total outstanding shares.[14] On the face of things Miller's fear that the business would be unprofitable was justified. After the war the company did not prosper as it had done before and it was on the verge of bankruptcy a number of times. Nor was its credit standing all that it might have been. Conservative business men were not impressed by Carnegie's character. For example, Daniel Morrow and John Stevenson refused to be partners because they thought Carnegie was too flighty.[15] Perhaps the company would have gone under had not Carnegie made a fortunate speculation in oil lands in Pennsylvania, the oil boom being in full swing at the time. He, with Mr. William Coleman, bought some oil wells on the Storey Farm for $40,000 from which they realized in one year a "million dollars in cash and dividends."[16] This money put the firm on its feet. The expansion of railroads after the war also gave them a greater market for their products. A strike occurred in the mills and the management imported German laborers as strike-breakers. Incidentally the management procured valuable technical assistance. Borntraeger, one of the strike-breakers, devised a means of detecting waste in the heating of materials which gave the company some advantage over its competitors through the savings that followed.[17] Zimmer, another strike-breaker, introduced a new rolling-device which became quite profitable. Borntraeger became a partner and ultimately a millionaire. Zimmer became a foreman and was worth possibly $100,000 when he died.

By 1870 there was a great demand for pig iron. A larger enterprise might prosper and money could be gained from the organization. In 1870 Klóman, Phipps, Andrew Carnegie, and Thomas Carnegie organized the firm of Kloman, Carnegie and Company which was to build blast furnaces and start manufacturing pig iron.[18] Phipps was instrumental in starting the use of flue-cinder and employing chemists,[19] which resulted in considerable economies for the company. Shortly thereafter, Kloman left the firm, and although through his technical proficiency he had done much toward developing the business and making it profitable, his withdrawal deprived him of the fruits of victory. He did not become a millionaire.

No sooner was this organization completed than a new one was started for the purpose of making steel rails and getting into, at the first, an industry that seemed to have a profitable future. Carnegie was not certain that the Bessemer process of steel making would be profitable. In fact it was not until he had seen its successful operation in England that he was willing to engage in the manufacture of steel.[20] And while he was trying to make up his mind as to whether or not he should try the process, William Coleman and T. M. Carnegie proceeded to organize a steel plant.[21]

Coleman persuaded David A. Stewart, president of the Pittsburgh Locomotive Works, and John Scott, a director of the Allegheny Valley Railroad, to go into the project; their railroad connections were desirable for the new concern. David McCandless, a friend of Tom Carnegie and a prominent merchant and banker of Pittsburgh, was persuaded to enter the enterprise, and he insisted that his friend William P. Shinn be taken in. Kloman also succeeded in getting into this new concern. Coleman, Scott, McCandless, and Tom Carnegie bought a homestead tract in Pittsburgh, converted it into building lots, and made considerable profit on the deal.[22] They were in good financial condition to enter the steel business. Andrew Carnegie returned from Europe with $150,000 which he had acquired as a commission for the sale of some bonds for a new railroad. He was willing to invest this and some more in the new concern. The firm of Carnegie, McCandless and Company was organized with a capital of $700,000. Andrew Carnegie was the largest investor, having contributed $250,000.

Shortly thereafter the name of the company was changed and the capitalization increased. It was called the Edgar Thompson Steel Company, Ltd., with a capital of one million dollars. Before the new plant was completed the depression of 1873 involved the firm in great financial difficulty. The high credit standing of McCandless, Stewart, and Scott pulled the firm through. Another fortunate event for the new company was a strike in the Cambria Iron Mills at Johnstown. Carnegie induced William Jones to leave the Cambria plant, and a large number of skilled steel workers followed Jones to the new company. The acquisition of this skilled workmanship, when skilled steel workers were relatively rare, had not a little to do with the success of the new company.[23] The company also received railroad rebates.

After the new concern got under way quarrels between the

partners increased. In many cases the quarrels ended in increased control of the company by Carnegie. Kloman had left Kloman, Carnegie and Company, but he was still interested in the Lucy Furnace Company, a concern in which Andrew Carnegie was also interested. Kloman was not trained in the intricacies of high finance. He invested in a concern organized to mine and smelt iron ore, The Escanaba Furnace Company. The concern was of unlimited liability. When it failed during the panic of 1873 some of the other investors in the Lucy Furnace Company thought Kloman might drag them into bankruptcy. Andrew Carnegie offered Kloman full partnership in the Carnegie properties if Kloman "would make a voluntary assignment and get a judicial discharge." Kloman agreed to this and was able to make a settlement of fifty cents on the dollar. Instead of full partnership Carnegie offered Kloman an interest of $100,000 in the various enterprises, to be paid out of profits. Kloman was dissatisfied with this and demanded complete reinstatement in all the Carnegie enterprises.[24] He could not enforce his demands and withdrew from the enterprise in great bitterness. Carnegie acquired Kloman's interest of $50,000 in the Edgar Thompson Company. Carnegie wanted to buy out Mr. Coleman and hoped to do so.[25] A disagreement arose as to the competency of a manager in the mills. The two could not agree, so, Carnegie states, "I had therefore to take over Mr. Coleman's interest."[26]

The Lucy Furnace Company had been organized to supply the Edgar Thompson Company with pig iron. There was disagreement as to the price to be paid the Lucy Furnace Company for pig iron. Some of those in the Edgar Thompson thought that the Furnace Company should not have any undue advantage because of its close connection with the Edgar Thompson Company. As a result of the disagreement Phipps and T. M. Carnegie sold half of their stock in the Edgar Thompson Company to Andrew Carnegie. It was mentioned that failure for the firm in 1873 was imminent. Certain new partners had credit which enabled the company to get some funds. Other funds were acquired by a bond issue. If these bonds were converted into stock after the depression the controlling stockholders might lose control. They decided to retire the bonds with cash. The concern was considered a risky one. Nearly all were willing to take cash while they could get it. Thompson, himself, died before the bonds were retired, but his executors willingly took cash. Only Gardner McCandless insisted that his bonds be converted into stock. John Scott might have demanded stock had he not had a quarrel with Carnegie, which made him anxious to get out. Carnegie bought him out and shortly afterward bought out McCandless.

The chairman of the board died. Shinn expected to be given the position. Carnegie decided his brother Tom Carnegie should have the job. A quarrel ensued and Shinn was invited to leave. Shinn thought he might as well leave, but there was disagreement over the settlement. The dispute finally got into court and, although Carnegie thought Shinn should receive but $105,000 for his share in the company, the court finally decided that Shinn had something under $200,000 coming to him.[27]

The company was changed into Carnegie Brothers and Company in 1880, with a capitalization of five million dollars. It included the Edgar Thompson Company, the Lucy Furnace Company, and the Union Iron Mills. With the withdrawal of Shinn, Scott and McCandless, Andrew Carnegie had by far the largest control in the company. The next largest stockholders were Henry Phipps and T. M. Carnegie. Two years after the Carnegie Company was organized the owners of it got control of the Homestead steel works, one of their strongest competitors. It seems that the Homestead mills had some labor troubles and had signed a contract with a union which had cut into the company's profits considerably. When a period of falling prices ensued some of the stockholders were willing to sell out to any one who would take the property off their hands. Although business was bad at the time, the Carnegie group could easily use the added equipment and incidentally rid themselves of an embarrassing rival.

At about the same time a further acquisition by the Carnegie Company brought into the steel industry another of the so-called captains of industry, Mr. Henry Clay Frick. In many respects Mr. Frick's rise to importance in the industry was similar to that of Carnegie and his associates. According to Carnegie, Frick "had proved his ability by starting as a poor railway clerk and succeeding."[28] As a matter of fact Frick started as a comparatively poor farmer's son. He first worked as a clerk in a country store and then became a bookkeeper in his grandfather's flouring mill and distillery at Broad Fork, Pennsylvania. His biographer tells us that, like not a few others of his contemporaries, he was anxious for pecuniary success and was determined to "get a 'good business training'; and time for diversion from that definite aim could not be spared."[29]

Frick was living in a region where some start had been made in the coke business, and he was early impressed with its possibilities, particularly when the needs of the expanding steel industry were considered. Like other of his contemporaries he made his first big business deal on borrowed money. He purchased one hundred and twenty-three acres of coal land when he was scarcely past twenty-one. Presumably he financed this deal either through loans from the executors of his mother's estate or through loans from his partner, J. S. R. Overholt.[30] Although his father had, according to the proud phrase of the son, "managed to bring up six children without running into debt," the son himself was not opposed to indebtedness. He induced his father to endorse his notes, which he peddled to all the farmers around, "often hitching up at dawn and driving all over the country and coming back at night with pockets full of greenbacks."[31] This money he used in further purchases of coal land. After the firm of Frick and Company was organized with Tinstman and Rist as partners, Frick decided that more credit was needed. There was difficulty in getting people to lend money without having them desire control in the company. He thought it best to establish the credit of the firm by demonstrating its ability to borrow money from outside sources.

He applied for a loan from T. Mellon and Sons, the most prominent bankers in Pittsburgh. The elder Mr. Mellon was a prudent, thrifty Scotchman who had acquired something of a fortune through fortunate speculations in real estate. He launched out into the banking business in 1870 at a time when business was good and made large profits.[32] Frick called on Mellon and said he would like to borrow $10,000 for six months at 10 per cent, with which to build fifty coke ovens. He got the loan, much to people's amazement. It has even been suggested that he received the money because he possessed the proper economic virtues. For example, John Moody says, "The banker had himself worked up from poverty; he liked the honest, bright face of the youth and was impressed with his sincerity and intelligence."[33] Another interpretation is, Judge Mellon "had invested all of his loose means in coal lands which might be enhanced in value immensely if some zealous and intelligent young man should devise at his own expense a 'coking process' that should prove indispensable to the steel industry."[34] In fact, the loan was increased to $20,000. And although one investigator said the loan was too risky, Mellon insisted on continuing in the enterprise.

During the depression of 1873 Frick decided it would be cheaper to continue operations than to close down the works entirely. He personally went to Pittsburgh to get what orders there were and continued making coke. He also continued acquiring more lands at greatly reduced prices. A railroad had been planned to connect with the B. and O., to facilitate the marketing of coke. The depression had frightened the stockholders of the railroad and they were in need of as much money as they could get. Frick saw them all and got options on their stock. He then took these options to the B. and O. and suggested that it buy out the feeder line. It did so, later gaining great profits from the connection and giving Frick a check for $50,000, a large part of which "he promptly invested in more lands and more ovens."

In 1878 he sold an interest in the business to E. M. Ferguson, a Pittsburgh capitalist, which gave Frick additional capital to expand his holdings. When the depression had drawn to an end the new firm was in a position to start operations immediately. The steel mills were demanding great quantities of coke, and it seems that the Frick Company was producing about eighty per cent of the entire output of the Connelsville region. At the close of the year 1879 Frick was worth a million dollars.[35]

Judge Mellon saw in Frick the traits that he considered

essential to great success in business. At least he told his son
Andrew:

> That young man has great promise. He is very careful in
> making statements, always exact, and wholly reliable. He is also
> able, energetic, industrious, resourceful, self-confident, somewhat
> impetuous, and inclined to be daring on his own account, but so
> cautious in his dealing with others disposed to take chances that
> I doubt if he would make a successful banker. If he continues
> along his own line as he has begun, he will go far unless he over-
> reaches. That is his only danger.[36]

Frick was on friendly terms with Thomas Carnegie and incidentally was interested in keeping close contact with such a large
market for coke as the Carnegie Brothers and Company afforded.
Carnegie was interested in a regular supply of coke. Consequently an organization was formed to take advantage of this
situation. The H. C. Frick Coke Company was formed to take
over the older company's assets and liabilities and to provide more
capital through the sale of stock. The original holders of stock
in the company were Andrew Carnegie, Thomas Carnegie, Henry
Phipps, H. C. Frick, E. M. Ferguson, Walter Ferguson, Carnegie
Brothers and Company Ltd., H. C. Frick and Company. The
actual ownership of the 40,000 shares of stock that were issued
was as follows: Fergusons, 23,654; Frick, 11,846; Carnegie
group, 4,500. Although Frick had reduced his percentage of
interest in the company he had greatly strengthened the credit
position of the firm through this alliance and had provided some
$325,000 in cash. Frick was anxious for additional capital for
immediate expansion, a policy with which Thomas Carnegie
agreed but of which Andrew disapproved.[37] The expansion Frick
referred to was the purchase of certain coal lands that he owned
and which had not been included in the H. C. Frick Coke Company. The transaction was no doubt profitable to Frick and
Carnegie decided he would not lose by it since it gave him
(Carnegie) a greater control of the coke company.

The collusive control of the coke company did not mean that
the partners were entirely co-operative in their plans and management of the company. Many of their disagreements arose over

management and labor problems. In 1887 a labor strike was called in the coke industry. Frick wanted to hold out against the union and break the strike, but he did not have a sufficiently strong interest on the board to carry out his plans. The Carnegie group felt a strike would be disastrous. They would be forced to bank their furnaces when they could least afford it. Consequently they reversed the policies suggested by Frick. Frick resigned as president of the company and proposed selling out to Carnegie. No definite action was taken, but it later developed that Frick was right about the labor situation. The other companies won the fight against the union, but the Carnegies had given in and were paying 12½ per cent higher wages than their competitors.[38]

When Frick's prophecy came true Carnegie was less willing to see him leave the company, as he might be able to prevent such another mistake. At any rate Frick was re-elected president of the company. In 1889 Carnegie offered him a partnership in the Carnegie Company. Frick acquired a 2 per cent interest in the company which increased to 11 per cent in the next three years, and he became chairman of the company.

Although not a little of the success of the Carnegie Company resulted from the company's connection with the Pennsylvania Railroad, Carnegie felt that the railroad was charging "exorbitant and discriminatory rates" for carrying steel products. Apparently the railroad was making all it could out of the steel industry. Carnegie suggested "that solitary confinement would be a good thing for railroad officials."[39] Not only did this controversy indicate how business men who were once friendly could become estranged when their pecuniary interests differed, it also revealed further conflict between the partners. Frick wrote Carnegie that his attack on the Pennsylvania Railroad was wrong and that he would deprecate its renewal.[40] He felt that their interests in the future were tied up with the railroad and it would be folly to break from them. Carnegie finally gave in to his chairman and evinced confidence in him.

The firm showed good profits and the chairman continued in a policy of expansion. In 1890 he succeeded in acquiring the Duquesne Steel Company, a strong competitor. The Duquesne

Company used a direct rolling process of rail-making which made a technically better rail than the Carnegie Company was making. So efficient had the company become that one of the Carnegie partners stated, "They were a thorn in our flesh and they reduced the price of rails."[41] At one time they were members of the rail pool, but the Carnegies were strong enough to get the poorer orders shifted on to the Duquesne Company which hampered their expansion. They had the further disadvantage of poor financial connections. They could not readily procure new capital. On top of this the sudden development of labor disputes further embarrassed them so that they were in a favorable disposition for selling. Frick obtained the property for one million dollars of Carnegie Brothers and Company bonds. When the bonds fell due the plant had paid for itself six times over.[42]

The partners had been running three different companies: The Carnegie, Phipps and Company, The Carnegie Brothers and Company, and the Frick Coke Company, and it was thought there would be some advantage in merging. The separate organizations had been desirable from the financial point of view. "That is, one Carnegie company selling to another was able to discount the notes it received in payment; so that the transaction had all the banking advantages of an outside trade."[43] But the companies were becoming so profitable that this type of financial assistance was no longer necessary. If emergencies did arise the Carnegie companies could fall back on the good credit standing of the Frick Coke Company.

A merger was agreed to by the twenty-two partners, and the physical properties of the older concerns were sold to the new company, The Carnegie Steel Company, Limited, capitalized at $25,000,000. The securities of the absorbed companies were exchanged for securities in the new organization. "The transaction, in effect, was a mere increase in capital from the original $5,000,-000 to $25,000,000 through what amounted to a 400 per cent share dividend."[44] The extra $20,000,000, which was created by a bookkeeping transaction in the hope that there would be increased earnings in the future, was distributed among the partners so that the proportion of stock held by each individual would remain the same. Only Carnegie, Phipps, and Frick were independent shareholders. The others were called "debtor partners." That is, they owed the company for the shares allotted to them, and these shares were eventually paid for out of earnings. The process by which these "junior partners" were selected can only be guessed at. Sometimes, as in the case of Borntraeger, the selection was on the basis of technical proficiency. Sometimes promotions through the various positions in the mills culminated in a partnership. Others were promoted for following Carnegie's advice about attracting the attention of one's superior officers. It has been said that George Lauder, one of the junior partners, acquired his position because he was able to tell Carnegie the meaning of the expression, "modulus of elasticity."[45] Carnegie explains Lauder's partnership on the ground that he invented a coal-washing process.[46] Another possible explanation is that Lauder became partner because he was Carnegie's cousin.

Charles M. Schwab became conspicuous in the steel industry at the time of the famous Homestead Strike in 1892. He had entered the employment of the Edgar Thompson Steel Works in 1880 at the age of eighteen. He seemed to be particularly successful in managing men and getting them to work without feeling they were under the whip of a "driver." This reputation he had acquired is the reason usually given for his continued promotions. He finally became assistant manager. When the Homestead works were established Carnegie selected him as superintendent. He was later placed in charge of the Edgar Thompson, and when the Homestead strike occurred he was brought back as the one best able to keep the men in line and prevent further difficulties and fights from arising.

The Homestead strike was a further occasion for disagreements among the partners. Carnegie was accused of shirking responsibility in the strike and of making statements for popular consumption regarding labor relations with no intention that these statements would be put into practice. His partners accused him of running off and not facing the ensuing outbreak of hostilities.[47] Frick earned the reputation of being "hard-boiled" in his attitude toward the union. A representative of the Republican National

Committee called on him during the strike to see if Frick would not try to patch up the struggle since a prolonged fight against the union might endanger the prospects of a Republican victory in the coming Presidential election. But Frick was a "Bitter-ender." He exploded to the astonished politician: "Yes, if it takes all summer and all winter and all next summer and all next winter. Yes, even my life itself. I will fight this thing to the bitter end. I will nèver recognize the union, never, never!" He went on to say he believed what he was doing was really in the true interests of the men themselves. The Amalgamated Association, he said, was one of the most tyrannous bodies on the face of the earth. He had put up with it as long as he could and proposed to stand it no longer.[48]

While others connected with the ownership and management of the company might agree with Mr. Frick's sentiments, they soon realized that such talk, at least in public, would not do the company any good. Especially since Carnegie had made somewhat different remarks in public. Schwab seemed to be the proper person for the center of the stage at this point in the proceedings. There was considerable agreement with the view that "young Mr. Schwab's zeal, charm and vivid personality had proved of inestimable value in restoring good feeling between the various groups so recently incensed at one another."[49] Not that Schwab's personality settled the conflict. But it was thought a good business asset. Mr. Schwab was retained and continued to advance.

A further expansion of the Carnegie Company brought in another man who was to make his fortune from the industry— Henry W. Oliver. His start was orthodox; that is, his first efforts were as a messenger boy in the Pittsburgh telegraph office.[50] He was something of a speculator in steel and iron manufacture and had become a member of a large Pittsburgh firm of plow and shovel manufacturers.

Supplies of iron ore were of course essential to steel manufacture. The rumor that J. D. Rockefeller was investing in ore lands in the Lake Superior region attracted the attention of eager money-makers. Oliver succeeded in acquiring some ore land. In 1892 he organized the Oliver Mining Company to operate the first mine opened on the famous Mesaba range. Frick suggested to Oliver that they go into the mining enterprise together. Such an arrangement would give the steel company an assured source of iron ore and would give the mine a sure market for its product. Carnegie opposed the combination because it seemed too hazardous. He wrote Frick:

> Oliver's ore bargain is just like him—nothing in it. If there is any department of business which offers no inducement, it is ore. It never has been very profitable, and the Massaba (sic) is not the last great deposit that Lake Superior is to reveal.[51]

Frick, however, went ahead and made an arrangement whereby the Carnegie ore interest would not cost a cent. Oliver agreed to Frick's proposal "to give the Carnegie Company one half the stock of the Oliver Mining Company, conditioned on a loan of half a million dollars, secured by a mortgage on the ore properties, to be spent in development work."[52]

While Carnegie was still protesting the arrangement, Frick and Oliver completed it. They made an arrangement with Rockefeller's managers to lease his properties on a royalty basis of twenty-five cents a ton (other mine owners were getting sixty-five cents a ton) "in consideration of a guaranteed output of 600,000 tons a year, to be shipped over the Rockefeller transportation system." To the Carnegie-Oliver iron interests the arrangement meant a visible saving of $27,000,000.[53]

The reduced royalties permitted a reduced selling price at the Lake Erie docks. Other mining companies without the reduced royalties and companies that did not control transportation systems were faced with prospects of huge losses. Their stockholders were thrown into a panic and were anxious to be rid of their holdings. Frick and Oliver waited until the stock depression which they had encouraged seemed to be at its worst and then gathered options on the shares of the three most important companies. There was some question as to whether Carnegie would approve the purchases, but when he saw the favorable conditions under which the deal was proceeding he assented. The transaction was made possible by strong financial backing, an assured market for the ore, and the depression in the price of mining stock.[54]   Within two years the Carnegie-Oliver interests were able to acquire "sufficient additional lands to give them exclusive ownership of two thirds of the greatest high-grade Bessemer ore deposits in the world."[55]

There were further fortunate results.   The Carnegie Company was now in a position to make itself independent from the Pennsylvania Railroad by financing an independent line. Carnegie acquired the Pittsburgh, Shenango and Lake Erie Railroad.   The road was reorganized, renamed the Pittsburgh, Bessemer and Lake Erie, extended some forty-two miles so that the Carnegie had direct connections between the company's docks at Conneaut and Pittsburgh.[56]   Besides the railroad, a fleet of six vessels on the lakes was acquired and a new subsidiary was formed, The Pittsburgh Steamship Company, to take over these shipping interests.   The Carnegie Company was virtually independent as regards raw materials and transportation facilities.   It became the strongest steel company and was in a position to further enhance profits by dictating terms to companies less advantageously placed.

Mr. Frick recommended securing a large body of ore because of the effect it would have "upon the guarantee made us, by the Rockefeller party, that our ore shall be as low as any other Mesaba ore at Lake Superior ports.   The possession of a large body of ore in the Gogebic Range will strengthen our position, in holding the Rockefeller people down to low freight rates from the Mesaba Range."[57]

The strong position of the company would also enable it to make favorable contracts with sellers of steel materials.   For example a contract was made with the American Tin Plate Company of New Jersey regarding the price of steel plates.   The following agreement was added to the contract:

Sellers agree, so long as the Buyers perform their part of this Contract "They will not sell to any competitive person or Company in the United States, Tin or Black Plate Bars of the character covered by this Contract;" and Sellers agree "Not to enter into competition with the Carnegie Steel Company, Limited, in any of the products which the Carnegie Steel Company, Limited, manufactures, during the life of this contract."[58]

It would seem that great strength as well as virtue were necessary to increased profits, or rather the maintenance of profits. Nor were these contracts always respected. They were often of little help to the company that was not strong enough to force the other party to the contract to observe them.[59]

In a concern organized after the manner of the Carnegie Company, where there were a few large owners and a number of junior partners, especially when the junior partners were having their stock bought for them by the company, the fortunes of these junior partners were dependent upon how well they were regarded by the controlling power, that is, the majority owner. In any internal conflicts they could be counted on to side with the controlling power. Frick and Carnegie each had rather definite ideas how things should be run and were not always in entire agreement. It seemed that Carnegie would not object if Frick left the company entirely. A conflict arose which provided the occasion for the final break.

The Carnegie Company had been getting its coke from the Frick Coke Company at greatly reduced prices. Some of the minority stockholders in the Frick concern objected to this because they had other properties they wanted to help besides the Carnegie Company. Frick became the spokesman for this group. It seems that Carnegie had made a three-year agreement with Frick for the coke at $1.35 a ton. He suddenly discovered that if the market price dropped below $1.35 he might not have such a good bargain as he had thought. He sent Schwab to tell Frick that if the price dropped below $1.35 the Carnegie Company would pay the market price. Frick would not consider this proposal and considered the agreement off. Furthermore Frick was about to sell some land to the Carnegie Company, whereupon Carnegie accused him of making exorbitant profits out of the transaction.

Frick informed the Carnegie Company that "Harmony is so essential for the success of any organization that I have stood a great many insults from Mr. Carnegie in the past, but I will submit to no further insults in the future."[60] Consequently he resigned as a member of the Board of the Carnegie Company.

Of course in this situation the behavior of the junior partners was such as to suit the largest owner, regardless of their personal feelings in the matter. Mr. Schwab explained the position of the junior partners in a letter to Frick:

. . . I have gone into the matter carefully and am advised by disinterested and good authority that, by reason of his (Carnegie's) interest, he can regulate this matter to suit himself—with much trouble no doubt, but he can ultimately do so. I believe all the Junior members of the board and all the Junior Partners will do as he directs. Any concerted action would be ultimately useless, and result in their downfall. Am satisfied that no action on my part would have any effect in the end. We must declare ourselves. Under these circumstances, there is nothing left for us to do but obey, although the situation the board is thus placed in is most embarrassing.[61]

Carnegie owned a little more than half of the stock in the Frick Company, so at the next stockholders' meeting he increased the Board of Directors from five to seven, dropped two of the former Frick men and replaced them with Carnegie men. Six of the members of the directorate were managers of the Carnegie Company. Four of them had not previously been stockholders, so to make them eligible, each of them had five shares of stock put in his name. The new Board subsequently voted to the Carnegie Company a contract for all the coke at $1.35 a ton. The market price was then $3.50 a ton.[62] Moreover the contract was made retroactive so that the coke company owed the Carnegies $526,000.

The minority stockholders of the coke company brought suit and Carnegie tried to force Frick to sell out to him at a much lower price than the market value of Frick's holdings. When the controversy got into the courts the result was that Frick got some 60 per cent more for his holdings than he would had not the court intervened.

The controversy was bringing the two companies into disrepute in the industry, so it was finally decided that things could be patched up by a merger of the Carnegie Company and the coke company. After much quibbling and discussion the Carnegie Company of New Jersey, capitalized at $160,000,000, was organized to take over the properties of the Carnegie Company and the Frick Coke Company. The three chief shareholders received the following securities:

	STOCK	BONDS
Andrew Carnegie	$86,382,000	$88,147,000
Henry Phipps	17,227,000	17,577,000
Henry C. Frick	15,484,000	15,800,000

The remainder went to some sixty junior partners and heirs of deceased members of the firm.[63] The new Carnegie Company had scarcely lived a year when it was taken into the United States Steel Corporation, and the numerous partners became millionaires by the transaction. But before the formation of this new corporation is considered let us observe one or two individuals who were becoming prominent in steel circles but who were not of the Carnegie lineage.

Perhaps it would be well to say a word about the general situation which was bringing the formation of a greater corporation into the realm of possibility and according to some, of necessity.

The newly formed Carnegie Company was about to expand along new lines. At least it had announced its intention to construct a $12,000,000 tube plant upon land recently acquired at Conneaut on Lake Erie. This seemed dangerous to the trade, particularly the National Tube Company, backed by J. P. Morgan & Company. Carnegie seemed ready for a period of aggressive competition against other steel companies. At least he sent the following message from Scotland to his partners:

If I were czar (of the Carnegie Company), I would make no dividends upon common stock, save all surplus, and spend it for a hoop-and-cotton-tie mill, for wire and nail mills, for tube mills, for lines of boats upon the Lakes for our manufactured articles, and to bring back scrap, etc. . . . Put your trust in the policy of attending to your own business in your own way and running your mills full, regardless of prices, and very little trust in the efficacy of artificial arrangements with your competitors, which have the serious result of strengthening them if they strengthen you. Such is my advice.[64]

Perhaps the aggressive tactics announced and threatened by Carnegie had something to do with an arrangement looking toward an amalgamation that would bring peace as well as profits to the various large interests, an arrangement that finally culminated in the formation of the United States Steel Corporation.

The Carnegie group was only one of the groups to be brought into the new combinations. Other groups were present and with them other wealthy men. Consider the careers of John W. Gates and Judge Elbert H. Gary.

Gary's career was not greatly different from many of his associates. His father was a farmer who had moved from Connecticut to Illinois and finally settled near Wheaton. The Gary family were good Methodists, had great respect for the homely virtues of industry, prudence, and thrift. Along with other farmers they hated corporate wealth, although Elbert seems to have overcome this prejudice at an early stage in his career. He was trained in the proper economic virtues and felt his destiny was in his own hands. He, like other of his contemporaries, was to be the judge of his own righteousness. His biographer reports him as saying, "I never allowed a teacher to punish me if I didn't think I deserved it."[65] This principle was retained in later years.

His career was undecided when Vallette and Cody, friends of his father, offered him a job in their law office. When Vallette moved to Chicago he offered Gary a position in a law firm there. Gary went there in 1871, but the great Chicago fire ruined the firm in which Vallette was a partner. Then he and Gary decided to start a law firm of their own.[66] Gary won a number of cases for prominent business men in and around Chicago. He explains these successes on the grounds of great industry. While other young lawyers were playing poker he was sitting up puzzling over ways to win his case. He also seems to have been unduly honest. His sister once came to the law office and started to take a few sheets of the firm's stationery. Gary reprimanded her for the attempted theft.[67]

Gary's reputation as a lawyer in Chicago increased, but his first connection with the steel industry resulted from his services to John W. Gates in amalgamating some wire factories. Gates sought Gary as one who could make the concern legal.

Gates, himself, did not vary from the pattern of the self-made man. There were some deviations in his later career which brought censure from J. P. Morgan and kept him out of some successful deals. He started as a poor boy, of course. His father was a farmer and instructed John in the economic virtues. At an early age he left the farm to make his fortune. He obtained a job as a salesman and was unusually successful. The concern for which he worked was manufacturing barbed wire to be sold to farmers for fencing. A Mr. Glidden had patented the manufacturing process and went into business with Ellwood, a hardware dealer. They bought their wire from Washburn and Moen, a firm in Worcester, Massachusetts. The business became so profitable that the Worcester firm suggested a partnership. Glidden was bought out and those left organized a partnership under the name of Ellwood and Washburn.[68]

Selling the goods was the main problem for the concern. Some of the cattlemen in the West did not think the barbed wire was strong enough to hold their cattle. Gates was hired to break down this "sales-resistance." He traveled about to country fairs, built corrals with his wire and demonstrated that cattle could not break through. His orders for wire increased; in fact, they increased so rapidly that he wondered if he were not wasting his time working for others. He decided to go into the business himself. The only obstacle to this venture was that the patents for the manufacturing process were controlled by Ellwood and Washburn. Gates's enterprising spirit overcame this obstacle by starting a small factory and calmly appropriating his former employers' patents for the manufacture of barbed wire. The firm of Ellwood and Washburn obtained an injunction against his operations in Missouri where he had started. This merely forced him to move his business into Illinois. The holders of the patents considered the matter and finally decided it would be easier to license Gates than it would be to fight him. After all, he was known to the farmers and he was getting their orders for fence wire. Consequently he was taken into the fold by his former employers.

But Gates had established five scattered factories, which were difficult to manage as a whole, competition from new firms was becoming severe, and price wars were frequent. A further amalgamation was thought desirable. Gates appealed to Gary for legal assistance in organizing the Consolidated Steel and Wire Company, capitalized at $4,000,000. Later, with the assistance of J. P. Morgan & Company, they attempted to organize the American Steel and Wire Company, to be capitalized at $80,000,-000, which would include practically the whole trade. The monopoly power of the company was the basis for the high capitalization. They were unable to complete the organization, so Gary organized a less ambitious concern called the American Steel and Wire Company of Illinois, capitalized at $24,000,000. Gates was not entirely satisfied with this concern, but he stayed with it, at least for a time.

Gates and Gary also figured in the organization of the Illinois Steel Company. Morgan was behind the organization; Gary was to handle the legal side of the organization because he had considerable information about the companies to be brought within the control of the new company. There was some question concerning Gates's position in the new concern. Although he controlled some securities there was thought of attempting to exclude him entirely. It was finally considered more prudent to have him in than to leave him out. He had the reputation of being a dangerous competitor.[69]

It was felt that the position of the new company could be still further strengthened by acquiring certain properties which would give it a stronger competitive position. In 1898 the Federal Steel Company was incorporated as a holding company to acquire the stocks of the Illinois Steel Company, the Minnesota Iron Company, the Lorain Steel Company, and the Elgin, Joliet, and Eastern Railway, a belt line operating about the city of Chicago. The authorized capitalization of the company was

$200,000,000. Gary later stated that thirty-one million of the actual capitalization (ninety-eight million) did not appear in the book values of the constituent companies.[70] Judge Gary was chosen the first president of the new company, but Gates was squeezed out entirely. Morgan had other interests which might be endangered if Gates was about and did unexpected things with the new concern. He was thought too much of a plunger for safety.[71]

When Gates found himself outside the Federal Steel Company he went to New Jersey and organized the American Steel and Wire Company (capital of ninety millions), which represented a combination of Western plants engaged in the manufacture of barbed wire, nails, and wire fencing. Gates stated that ten or fifteen millions of the capitalization represented "good will."[72] It included other industries, and there was fear lest it encroach on the field which the Federal Steel Company was expected to control. Gates was under the handicap of having no very strong financial backing. Yet the concern was quite profitable for a time as a result of pooling agreements and monopolistic control of certain parts of the steel industry. Prices were maintained at a gratifyingly high figure.

Due to the large size of these organizations and the great amount of capitalization, promotion of the organizations was frequently a specialized task. It provided a new source for large fortunes. Gates's greatest efforts were in promotion. Judge W. H. Moore was another connected with the steel industry whose efforts in promotion were liberally rewarded. The stock was freely watered to meet such payments. The American Steel Hoop Company, of which Moore was an officer, had a capitalization of $14,000,000 preferred and $19,000,000 common; the common stock was for "good will" (expectation of profits) and pay for the promoter.[73] Moore organized the American Tin Plate Company in 1898, the common stock of which was almost entirely "water."[74]

While the wave of combinations in the latter nineties was bringing fortunes to the promoters and controllers of the respective companies, a situation was developing that might prove dis-

astrous, or so it was thought.   The Carnegie Company was the
strongest of the large concerns.   The group of companies backed
by Morgan—Federal Steel, National Tube, and the American
Bridge Company—was strong and profitable, but Morgan had
other interests as well and was not anxious to experience a period
of cutthroat competition.   The Moore companies, American Tin
Plate, American Steel Hoop, and the National Steel, would probably be seriously embarrassed if their stocks slumped appreciably
on the market.   And Gates's American Steel and Wire Company
had no strong financial backing which would carry it through a
period of stringency.

Carnegie made the situation appear even more dangerous.
He announced the immediate construction of a $12,000,000 tube
plant at Conneaut.   This would imperil the National Tube Company.   He announced that a rod-mill would be erected at Pittsburgh.   This would encroach on the business of the American
Steel and Wire.   He also ordered the construction of a fleet of
ore-carrying steamers to operate on the Great Lakes.

To indicate that he was not bluffing he instructed his managers to

inform these people that we do not propose to be injured; on the
contrary, we expect to reap great gains from it; that we will
observe an "armed neutrality" as long as it is made our interest
to do so, but that we require this arrangement—then specify
what is advantageous for us, very advantageous, more advantageous than existed before the combination, and we will get it.
If they decline to give us what we want, then there must be no
bluff.   We must accept the situation and prove that if it is fight
they want, here we are, always ready.   Here is a historic situation for the managers to study—Richelieu's advice: "First, all
means to conciliate; failing that, all means to crush."[75]

Carnegie, perhaps, was actually afraid of threatened competition.   He had been anxious to retire for some time, so it is not
improbable that he offered this threat in order to force the others
to buy him out at higher prices in order to remove the danger of
his presence.   At any rate Gates and Schwab approached Morgan
to see if he would back a new combination.   He finally agreed to

do so and Schwab got from Carnegie the price he would be willing to take for his interest in the Carnegie Company. The
amount finally decided on was equivalent to a cash payment of
$447,000,000. Carnegie had previously offered his interests to
Frick and Moore for $157,000,000; he had also offered it to
Rockefeller for $250,000,000. The more important the Carnegie
property became for the success of a new combination, the higher
went the price.

The other concerns that were to be taken into the new organization found that the value of their property increased greatly
as soon as the menace of Carnegie was removed. They held out
for as much as possible. Gary was a close bargainer and attempted to force all of the constituent companies to his own price.
Gates held out for a considerable time and accepted the price
offered him only after Morgan and Gary threatened to build their
own wire mill and leave him out entirely.

Gary had more difficulty in buying Rockefeller's iron ore
properties at a satisfactory figure. Rockefeller became less and
less willing to sell as he discovered the necessity of his property
to the success of the new organization. Morgan and J. D. Rockefeller, Jr., are reported to have bargained over the price to be paid
without reaching an agreement. Young Mr. Rockefeller even
suggested that the property was not for sale. Rockefeller is reported to have said, "Mr. Morgan. . . . I have no information to the effect that he (my father) wishes to dispose of his ore
properties; in point of fact, I am confident that he has no such
desire."[76]

The price was too low. Rockefeller, Sr., told Frick that he
didn't want to stand in the way of a worthy enterprise, but, he
said, "I do frankly object . . . to a prospective purchaser
arbitrarily fixing an 'outside figure,' and I cannot deal on such a
basis. That seems too much like an ultimatum."[77] The result of
their conversation was that Frick named a figure $5,000,000
greater than the "outside figure" previously offered by Gary and
Morgan. Gary was upset; he called it a "prohibitive proposition," but there was nothing to do but accept.

The necessary properties were finally acquired, and the

United States Steel Corporation was launched with prospects for fine profits for those concerned with it. Some were becomingly modest in their demands for reward. For example, Mr. Morgan sent a circular to the stockholders in which he said, "It is proper to state that J. P. Morgan & Company are to receive no compensation for their services as syndicate managers beyond a share in any sum which ultimately may be realized by the syndicate."[78] This share amounted to the modest figure of about $62,500,000.[79]

After the concern was started, difficulties developed between the officers and the directors. Gary had definite ideas as to how the concern should be run.[80] Many of those connected with the control of the new corporation did not at first consider it a co-operative enterprise in the sense that they should not make money out of it at the expense of those who were not on the inside. There was considerable opposition to Gary's attempt to prevent speculation in the securities of the corporation on the basis of inside information.[81] More serious difficulties developed as to the power and authority different officers were supposed to have. Schwab, the president of the organization, did not think he should take orders from Gary, the president of the Board. At one time certain stockholders went to Morgan with a request that Gary should be removed from office. At length Schwab resigned as president in 1903 and the friction seemed to decrease.[82] The reason why it was thought advisable for Schwab to resign was his entanglement with a shipbuilding company that proved a failure. Carnegie charged Schwab with having turned his attention from "the manufacture of iron to the manufacture of securities"; the Outlook gently reprimanded him by saying he lacked moral ballast.[83]

Although the promoters and controllers of the new corporation had all entered millionairedom, profits from transactions with the corporation did not cease. The Tennessee Iron and Coal Company seems to have been sold to the corporation at a rather high figure.[84] The bond conversion plan also appeared to be a device by which certain individuals would reap profits at the expense of other investors in the corporation.[85]

With the organization of the United States Steel Corporation Andrew Carnegie withdrew from active business life. He followed the policy which he had recommended to successful money-makers, that is, undertook philanthropies. After acquiring a fortune one should assist less fortunate members of society. Carnegie frequently asserted that he wanted to die poor. He became greatly interested in furthering international peace and endowed an organization to accomplish that purpose. He was greatly interested in education and thought he could best further that cause by establishing libraries in towns and cities in the United States. He admired valor and self-sacrifice and established an endowment for rewards to be given to individuals who had imperilled their lives in saving the lives of others. The opera and museums were not omitted from his list of philanthropies. By such expenditures great fortunes were to aid society.

The United States Steel Corporation was thought to necessitate behavior on the part of its officers and controllers different from that which had characterized the managers of the Carnegie Company. Carnegie had been considered an unruly competitor. The new organization was interested in stabilizing prices rather than slashing prices. Furthermore the new Steel Corporation came into a world that was increasingly critical of large combinations. If the organization expected to continue attention had to be given to "public relations"; that is, adverse legislation had to be averted and too great censure from the public had to be avoided. This necessity is perhaps the explanation for Judge Gary's prominence in the new organization. Some years after the organization of the new corporation Judge Gary stated in a public address:

In the United States the door of opportunity for progress and prosperity is open to all; but to reap the full advantages one must be actuated by the principles of morality. . . . No one can successfully claim that ethical management in business will combat religious conduct or that the latter will be obnoxious to the former.[86]

Such pronouncements coming from an insider might possibly increase the good will of the company.

J. P. Morgan sometimes wanted to control interests and properties in a manner not entirely legal. On one of these occasions Gary told Morgan that if he knew the purposes Morgan had in mind he would see if they could not be carried through in a way that would satisfy the law.[87] Such services endeared Gary to Morgan. Furthermore Gary announced certain policies of the new Steel Corporation such as: The rights of customers must always be respected; employees are associates—not servants; no preferential right to inside information; humane competition instead of destructive; full and prompt publicity.[88] It was thought that if the corporation could acquire the reputation of being a "good" organization then there would be no reason for governmental interference. Despite Gary's show of co-operation with the government he was greatly chagrined and disappointed when Wickersham told him he would have to bring suit for the dissolution of the trust.[89] Gary felt that the government had not been quite fair to him. Such public zeal should be rewarded. Whereupon John·W. Davis asserted that the suit was for the dissolution of the Steel Trust, not for the dissolution of Judge Gary. But there was some compensation for the maintenance of good "public relations" since it was decided that the United States Steel Corporation was not an actual monopoly but only a potential monopoly. Gary's behavior was becoming more important for those corporations coming within the realm of governmental investigation or regulation.

The success of the millionaires in the oil and steel industries obviously cannot be explained in terms of greater economic virtue or even of less economic virtue than the less successful money-makers possessed. Their practice of thrift, prudence, and industry was certainly not greater than the thrift and industry of the colonial merchants in New England, but the fortunes they realized were much larger. On the other hand their "dishonesty" was probably not greater than that of the early business men in the West. Even the farmers had not been unknown to misrepresent the quality of the meat they were selling, to water the milk, or to fill their cattle with water in order to increase their weight and bring greater profits. The great success of the later business men seemed to be due to the changed conditions under which they carried on their activity.

The business man was no longer controlling and managing all the processes of his industry or trade and personally selling his goods to customers. There had been a great increase in the "industrial arts" which in the mechanical industries called for extensive machinery and its supervision by technical experts. The size of industry became larger, necessitating a greater division of labor. The supervision of technical processes became specialized and somewhat separated from the business end of the industry. Individual proprietorship and even the partnership began to disappear and be replaced by the corporate form of enterprise. Greater capital could be secured in this manner. The business men began to devote more and more of their attention to corporation finance. With the increased productive capacity of industry situations frequently developed where more profits could be realized by restricting production rather than by encouraging it. And emphasis was put on vendible wealth rather than serviceable goods. Furthermore, under the new corporate regime more and more attention had to be given to the maintenance of credit and strong financial connections.[90]

Obviously under the new conditions a man and his business were no longer synonymous. The individual had a specialized job in a large organization. Individual thrift was no longer an essential factor in corporation thrift. Under individual proprietorship, financing is carried on by individual borrowing which must be repaid. This necessitates saving by the individual. In the corporate form of enterprise financing is carried on by the issue of new securities. This means that the corporation "may simply draw to itself a part of the existing fund of capital, under conditions that make the transfer of capital permanent."[91] To be sure the corporation saves. Although estimates of savings are always subject to considerable error Dr. W. I. King's estimate is that almost half, about forty per cent of the annual savings of the country are made by corporations.[92] But savings by a corporation are not synonymous with individual savings. If the increase of net assets be taken as the test of savings, a corporation may save by acquiring new properties or extending its plant. When the Carnegie Company acquired the Duquesne Steel Co., bonds were issued to make the purchase. The bonds were paid for out of the earnings of the new company that had been acquired. This acquisition represented "saving" for the Carnegie Company, but the saving did not come from the pockets of Carnegie and his partners.

The money-makers were all ardent advocates and practicers of self-help, but it was self-help under new conditions. First of all there was concentrated devotion to the one goal of money-making. But under the new conditions attention had to be given to the maintenance of credit standing and the possibilities of getting a "backer" since the initial investments in many cases were relatively large. This meant the practice of such behavior as was thought would appeal to those with money to lend. Those who were in a strong financial position found that business opportunities increased tremendously. They could make their own terms as to when they would buy or sell. They could acquire valuable properties during a business depression when prices are generally low. The man who can establish his credit and obtain financial assistance at such times is the one who will profit.[93]

Another aspect of their money-making is that greatest success comes when attention is concentrated on corporation finance and what has been called a traffic in abstract property.[94] The traffic in abstract property is a matter of dealing in corporate securities. This does not mean merely speculation on the stock exchanges. Carnegie, for example, was opposed to such speculation. He said speculation "is a parasite feeding upon values, creating none."[95] But his own success depended on controlling the stock in the concerns with which he was associated. Controlling the voting stock he could then control the policies such as the contract governing the price to be paid the Frick Company for coke. Without such control over securities many avenues to profits would be closed. Properties may be acquired by the issue of securities, the securities to be paid for out of the earnings of the new property. The promotion of consolidations is financed frequently by a process of recapitalization, part of the new issue of securities going as profits to the promoters. Under the corporate organization one individual could easily be connected with a whole series of corporations. He might sell one corporation various necessary commodities or equipment handled by another corporation with which he was connected. Sometimes he could set the price to suit himself. And of course opportunities for speculation in the securities of the corporation on the basis of inside information were available.[96]

It was pointed out in connection with the oil industry that the most successful money-makers had little to do with the technical side of the industry. In the steel industry many individuals and companies that were most proficient technically did not attain the largest fortunes. Kloman, Zimmer, Jones, The Cambria Company, and the Duquesne Company were not successful money-makers. Inventiveness and technical skill were rather precarious roads to fortune.

After the organization of the United States Steel Corporation there was a tendency to curtail the amount of profit-making by insiders at the expense of the other members of the corporation. It was felt that such activity would put the corporation in a bad light with the public and possibly lead to its ultimate dissolution.

The careers of the successful money makers connected with the oil and steel industries suggest that behavior did not necessarily conform to the traditional conception of economic virtue. The new millionaires reinterpreted the virtues to fit their own needs. It remains to be shown how the virtues were used by both the successful and their critics and what further changes occurred in the interpretation of economic virtues.

FOOTNOTES FOR CHAPTER VI

[1] *The Autobiography of Andrew Carnegie*, pp. 34, 36.
[2] *Ibid.*, p. 63.
[3] *Ibid.*, pp. 71ff.
[4] *Ibid.*, p. 73.
[5] *Ibid.*, p. 79.
[6] *Ibid.*, p. 89.

[7] James H. Bridge, *The Inside History of the Carnegie Steel Company*, p. 14.

[8] *Ibid.*, pp. 4ff.; Autobiography of Carnegie, p. 130.

[9] *Ibid.*, p. 132.

[10] J. H. Bridge, *op. cit.*, p. 4.

[11] *Ibid.*, p. 5.

[12] H. N. Casson, *The Romance of Steel*, p. 75.

[13] Autobiography of Carnegie, p. 133; J. H. Bridge, *op cit.*, p. 21.

[14] *Ibid.*, p. 31.

[15] H. N. Casson, *op. cit.*, p. 87.

[16] Autobiography of Carnegie, p. 139. Bridge attributes the saving of the firm to money obtained by Miller in oil speculations in 1862, J. H. Bridge. *op. cit.*, p. 62.

[17] *Ibid.*, pp. 32-33; Autobiography of Carnegie, p. 136.

[18] J. H. Bridge, *op. cit.*, p. 55.

[19] *Ibid.*, pp. 64-65.

[20] Autobiography of Carnegie, pp. 185ff.

[21] J. H. Bridge, *op. cit.*, pp. 72ff.

[22] *Ibid.*, p. 76.

[23] *Ibid.*, p. 79; H. N. Casson, *op. cit.*, pp. 20ff.; J. H. Bridge, *op. cit.*, p. 74.

[24] J. H. Bridge, *op. cit.*, pp. 68ff.; Autobiography of Carnegie, pp. 194ff.

[25] J. H. Bridge, *op. cit.*, p. 117.

[26] Autobiography of Carnegie, p. 202. For the difficulties with Lucy Furnace Co. see J. H. Bridge, *op. cit.*, pp. 87, 119.

[27] J. H. Bridge, *op. cit.*, pp. 126ff.

[28] Autobiography of Carnegie, p. 205.

[29] George Harvey, *Henry Clay Frick, the Man*, p. 15.

[30] *Ibid.*, p. 31.

[31] *Ibid.*, p. 33.

[32] *Ibid.*, pp. 38ff.

[33] John Moody, *The Masters of Capital*, p. 48.

[34] G. Harvey, *op. cit.*, p. 41.

[35] *Ibid.*, ch. 4.

[36] *Ibid.*, p. 69.

[37] *Ibid.*, pp. 78-79.

[38] *Ibid.*, pp. 83-86.

[39] The Commercial and Financial Chronicle, 1889, Vol. 48, p. 5050.

[40] G. Harvey, *op. cit.*, p. 97.

[41] J. H. Bridge, *op. cit.*, p. 177.

[42] G. Harvey, *op. cit.*, p. 101.

[43] J. H. Bridge, *op. cit.*, p. 254.

[44] G. Harvey, *op. cit.*, p. 102.

[45] H. N. Casson, *op. cit.*, p. 147.

[46] Autobiography of Carnegie, p. 144.

[47] G. Harvey, *op. cit.*, pp. 163-166.

[48] *Ibid.*, p. 151.

[49] *Ibid.*, p. 181.

[50] Autobiography of Carnegie, p. 42; H. N. Casson, *op. cit.*, p. 118.

[51] J. H. Bridge, *op. cit.*, p. 259.

[52] *Ibid.*, p. 258.

[53] *Ibid.*, pp. 260-261.

[54] H. R. Mussey, *Combination in the Mining Industry*, p. 124.

[55] G. Harvey, *op. cit.*, p. 195.

[56] *Ibid.*, pp. 197, 198.

[57] J. H. Bridge, *op. cit.*, p. 264.

[58] *Ibid.*, p. 285.

[59] Carnegie was considered one of the worst offenders in breaking these agreements. Gary considered him a "cruel competitor." Ida Tarbell, *The Life of Elbert H. Gary*, p. 90; J. W. Gates averred that Carnegie was "a bull in a china shop."

[60] J. H. Bridge, *op. cit.*, p. 325.

[61] *Ibid.*, p. 327.

[62] *Ibid.*, p. 329.

[63] G. Harvey, *op. cit.*, p. 257.

[64] *Ibid.*, p. 259.

[65] Ida Tarbell, *The Life of Elbert H. Gary*, pp. 23, 32.

[66] *Ibid.*, pp. 41-42, 49.

[67] *Ibid.*, p. 62.

[68] *Ibid.*, pp. 74-75.

[69] *Ibid.*, p. 88.

[70] United States, *Report of the Industrial Commission*, 1901. Vol. I, p. 987.

[71] Ida Tarbell, *op. cit.*, p. 96.

[72] *Report of the Industrial Commission*. Vol. I, p. 1021.

[73] *Ibid.*, Vol. I, pp. 959, 962-963, 967.

[74] The Commercial and Financial Chronicle, Aug. 29, 1896; Oct. 10, 1896.

[75] Quoted in G. Harvey, *op. cit.*, p. 260.

[76] *Ibid.*, pp. 263-264.

[77] *Ibid.*, p. 265.

[78] Quoted in L. H. Haney, *Business Organization and Combination*, p. 309.

[79] This amount was realized on the sale of 649,987 shares of preferred stock and 649,988 shares of common. $25,000,000 provided the corporation by the syndicate and $3,000,000 organization expenses were deducted from the proceeds of the sale. *Report of the Commissioner of Corporations on the Steel Industry*, Part I, p. 244.

[80] Ida Tarbell, *op. cit.*, pp. 135-136.

[81] *Ibid.*, pp. 143-144.

[82] *Ibid.*, p. 150.

[83] The Outlook, Aug. 15, 1903, Editorial on Schwab.

[84] Testimony of Gary quoted in W. H. S. Stevens, ed. *Industrial Combinations and Trusts*, p. 309.

[85] W. Z. Ripley, *Trusts, Pools and Corporations*, pp. 228ff. There was some uncertainty as to just what the syndicate gained by the conversion plan, *Ibid*, pp. 260-262. The syndicate was to receive a 4% commission for the exchange. Assuming that the plan was imprudent the corporation paid the syndicate $6,-800,000 for raising $20,000,000 of cash; in other words, a commission of 34%. *Ibid.*, p. 266.

[86] Judge Gary, *Ethics in Business*, Address delivered at Northwestern University, Evanston, Ill., June 17, 1922.

[87] Ida Tarbell, *op. cit.*, p. 81.

[88] Judge Gary, *op. cit.*, p. 8.

[89] Ida Tarbell, *op. cit.*, pp. 234-235.

[90] Thorstein Veblen, *Absentee Ownership*, ch. 6.

[91] Political Science Quarterly, 1907. Vol. 22, pp. 236-237, A. S. Johnson, *Influences Affecting Thrift*.

[92] W. I. King, "The Net Volume of Savings in the United States," Journal of American Statistical Association Nov., Dec. 1922.

[93] Anna Youngman, *The Economic Causes of Great Fortunes*, ch. on The Rockefeller Fortune.

[94] G. P. Watkins emphasizes "abstract property" as a means to wealth. *The Growth of Large Fortunes*, American Economic Association, Proceedings, Nov. 1907; Mr. Veblen emphasizes the concentration on "vendible wealth." See *The Theory of Business Enterprise*, ch. 3.

[95] Autobiography of Carnegie, pp. 153-154.

[96] J. M. Clark indicates the opportunities for profits through disloyalty to the corporation, *Econ. and Modern Psychology*, J. P. E. XXVI, pp. 152-160.

CHAPTER VII

NEW DEVELOPMENTS IN ECONOMIC VIRTUES

UNDER the new conditions there was some fear lest the traditional virtues disappear. At the turn of the century there was a great increase in the number of corporations and "trusts." At the opening of the nineties there had been some falling off in the number of business consolidations. This seemed to be due to adverse legislation. By 1896 or 1897 the movement started again and continued with great optimism until about 1904. From 1890 to 1896 (inclusive) forty-seven "trusts" were formed with a total capitalization of $638,725,667. This does not include purely local combinations, foreign controlled combinations, or combinations with a capitalization below one million dollars. From 1897 to 1904 one hundred and ninety trusts were formed with a total capitalization of $5,325,154,000.[1] Many fortunes were made from these combinations, although the combinations themselves did not always become profitable.

At the same time it was becoming apparent that the wage earners in many of the industries were not so well off as spokesmen for society at large had suggested. J. A. Ryan, in 1903, estimated that $600 was the minimum for a "decent" standard of living for a family of five. In his study of about four million adult male workers in manufacturing and transport he concluded that about 51 to 85 per cent of these workers were receiving an inadequate wage for this decent standard of living.[2] The Census Bureau investigated three million workers in manufacturing. Two and one half million of these were men. Of these 62 per cent earned less than $12 a week. If they worked full time they could earn but $624 a year. Over one fourth of those over sixteen years of age earned less than $420, forty-six per cent earned less than $520, and over seventy per cent earned less than $780. The average yearly earning was $575.[3] Scott Nearing said one third of the male factory employees in Massachusetts earned less than $500, one half earned less than $600, and nearly three fourths earned less than $700. He estimated that five million industrial workers in the United States were earning annually only $600 or less.[4]

The laborer, of course, was no longer a handicraftsman working with his own tools. Hard work and thrift were not the sole determinants of his economic existence. His employment was dependent upon the needs and desires of corporate enterprise. The prospective business of the enterprise, a factor not entirely dependent upon the productivity of workers, was perhaps the determining factor in the management's judgment as to whether employment should continue or wages change. In the face of this uncertainty about employment and wages it would seem that thrift and savings were even more imperative than they had been under earlier conditions of work. But the same conditions that made thrift necessary also made it almost impossible. Wages were too low to start very much saving.[5]

The new conditions created various grievances and conflicts between different groups. As evidenced by the large number of strikes many of the workers were turning from individual self-help to collective action as a means of improving their economic position. This was becoming obvious to the population at large, particularly in the famous Pullman strike of 1894 and the equally famous anthracite coal strike of 1902. The earlier struggle of the farmers and other shippers against transportation rates continued; small business men struggled with large corporations; consumers complained about "trust made goods."

In spite of the changing conditions and the changed behavior of many groups the traditional virtues did not disappear. To be sure there was some attempt to formulate different economic virtues. The Socialist Party, organized in 1901 and gaining steadily throughout the decade, emphasized co-operation and the collective ownership of the means of production, and had little use for the traditional virtues. The Industrial Workers of the World, organized in 1904, aspired toward the formation of One Big Union of all industrial workers and a General Strike, and considered sabotage and solidarity economic virtues. A small group in religious circles advocated a type of morality which they deemed applicable to the changed economic conditions. They preached the "Social Gospel," a doctrine that made salvation dependent upon a proper social and economic environment rather than on mere individual self help. Their influence was not immediately extensive. These various interpretations did not seem to be widely held.

Many of those who were distressed by the new conditions, particularly the farmers and the "independent business men," appealed to the traditional virtues as an argument against the new conditions. They felt they were being ruined by corporate wealth and "trusts." It was no longer possible for one to get ahead by his own efforts and the practice of the traditional virtues. The analysis suggested the remedy. Trusts should be abolished and economic activity should be brought back to what were thought to be pre-monopolistic conditions.

Anti-trust legislation appeared during the last ten or twelve years of the nineteenth century. In 1889 Kansas, North Carolina, Tennessee, and Michigan passed anti-trust laws. South Dakota, Kentucky, and Mississippi followed in 1890; then came North Dakota, Oklahoma, Montana, Louisiana, Illinois, Minnesota, Missouri, and New Mexico in 1891. Between 1893 and 1898 anti-trust statutes were passed by Wisconsin, Alabama, Arkansas, New York, Ohio, South Carolina, Texas, and Utah. The Federal government felt the pressure of anti-trust feeling and passed the Sherman Anti-Trust Act in 1890.

This legislation was passed in the name of the traditional virtues. The Independent Farmer was considered an American institution and self-help was glorified. If independence and self-help were to be preserved then, they argued, the trusts must be broken up.

Chief Justice Ryan of the Supreme Court of Wisconsin, addressing the University of Wisconsin in 1873, declared:

Already, here at home, one great corporation has trifled with the sovereign power, and insulted the State. There is grave fear that it, and its great rival, have confederated to make partition of the State and share it as spoils. . . . The question will arise, and arise in your day, though perhaps not fully in mine: "Which shall rule—wealth or man; which shall lead—money or intellect; who shall find public stations—educated and patriotic freemen, or the feudal serfs of corporate capital?"

John Sherman, introducing in Congress the Anti-Trust bill that bears his name, said:

They had monopolies and mortmains of old, but never before such giants as in our day. You must heed their appeal (the people of the United States) or be ready for the socialist, the communist, and the nihilist. Society is now disturbed by forces never felt before. . . .

And Senator George exclaimed in the debate on the bill:

They (the trusts) pursue unmolested, unrestrained by law, their ceaseless round of peculation under the law, till they are fast producing that condition in our people in which the great mass of them are the servitors of those who have this aggregated wealth at their command.[6]

It was feared that the trusts were producing conditions in which self-help and independence could not be practiced. And individuals connected with trusts were thought to be gaining wealth without practicing the traditional virtues. Ida Tarbell's and H. D. Lloyd's works have been mentioned as stressing this aspect of millionaires' careers. Many other books were written to prove this thesis. An economist some years later listed the "dishonest" and "unfair" methods by which wealth was gained. Local price cutting; operation of "bogus" independents; maintenance of fighting brands and fighting ships to be used to undercut competitors; exclusive sales and purchase agreements; rebates and preferential contracts; acquisition of exclusive or dominant control of machinery or goods used in the manufacturing process; manipulation of securities on the stock market; blacklists, boycotts, and whitelists; espionage and use of detectives; coercion, threats, and intimidation; these were some of the tactics employed by "big business."[7] Some of the observers of this process during the opening decade of the twentieth century thought these were the only means by which "big business" prospered.

Since these practices were not thought consistent with the

traditional virtues it was felt that here was one more reason for abolishing trusts. Those people should receive wealth who were independent, honest, thrifty and industrious. This criticism of trusts and the "new plutocracy" was conservative in the sense that the critics hoped to bring economic affairs back to the conditions that presumably prevailed in the earlier days. The criticism was not against the capitalist as such but against any economic organization that seemed to have monopoly power. The "muckrakers," such as Ida Tarbell, Lincoln Steffens, and Ray Stannard Baker, did not confine their attention to big business alone. Labor unions were criticized as well.[8]

Since large sections of the American populace seemed to cherish so dearly the traditional virtues, the wealthy were not long in adding to the chorus. Far from being opposed to the traditional virtues it was by these very virtues that they had succeeded. It seemed to them self-evident that great wealth was the accompaniment and result of thrift, industry and self-help. Carnegie's "Gospel of Wealth" and Rockefeller's pious reverence for the homely virtues have already been mentioned. Others rapidly added their testimony.

In a symposium on The Concentration of Wealth, Russell Sage said:

To rail against the accumulation of wealth is to rail against the decrees of justice. The whole thing is governed by the principle of autonomy. Intelligence, industry, honesty and thrift produce wealth, and those who possess such qualities are best fitted for its custody. So long as some men have more sense and more self-control than others just so long will such men be wealthy, while others will be poor.[9]

Charles M. Schwab stated the situation slightly differently. He said:

The man whom you hear say he "never had a chance" lacks something. He lacks that indefinable something that stands for success, and if you look far enough you'll find that something to be a capacity and a disposition for hard work. The only luck I ever had was to be born with good mental powers and a good physical constitution that thrived on the hardest kind of work. I had enough hardships and trials. I would not give up the experience of a boyhood barren of luxuries and paved with obstacles for any amount of money.[10]

If the wealthy possessed the economic virtues it easily followed that the poor had the economic vices. D. O. Mills, founder of the famous Mills Hotels, observed that "The most wasteful and extravagant people in the world to-day are the poor of our American cities."[11]

Henry L. Doherty suggested that thrift was the sure method of getting ahead. He said:

If it were possible for me to double the income of all our employees, the good I could do in that way would be less than if I could imbue them with an earnest desire and purpose to save and invest their money.[12]

Schwab appealed to the value of individual effort as an argument against labor unions. He said:

I would not want to belong to a labor organization. It puts all men, no matter what their ability, in the same class of work, on exactly the same level. If I were a better workman—quicker, smarter—than the other men, I would want to reap the benefit. I would not want to be put in the class with the poorer men, which they must do. . . . As a workingman I would not advance, and I would not be able to show superior ability over any other if I were in an organization.[13]

Just as the business men had used the virtues of self-help and private initiative against the farmers at an earlier time, the same virtues were now beginning to be used by the newer group of business men against the wage earners.

The "self-made" man was so extensively advertised that he sometimes has been considered a peculiarly American phenomenon. Means were taken to see that he was adequately presented to the public. An example will illustrate this. A magazine was started to attain that aim. It was called "The Successful American" and was published from 1900 to 1909. The magazine was not sold directly to the public but was distributed to other magazines and newspapers with the hope that it would be used as an authentic work of reference. According to the editors the magazine was

"Devoted to the Achievements of, and Containing Biographical and Character Sketches, together with Portraits of Representative Successful Americans." The nature of these sketches may be inferred from the following captions, representative of the bulk of the articles in the magazine:

Hugh McGowan—From Farm Boy to Street Railway Magnate and Millionaire.

Thomas W. Kennedy—He Began Life as a Poor Boy in Ohio and Achieved Success and Prosperity by Hard Work.

Alfred J. Major—Iron Clerk in the Pencoyd Iron Works He Has Risen to His Present Position.

Roswell P. Flower—A Country Boy's Career from Farm to Capital.

In short, the successful money-makers were using the traditional economic virtues to explain and defend their wealth. In doing so they aligned themselves with Puritanism, which was still influential in the thinking of the Americans, and made success synonymous with virtue and failure with vice.

However eloquent these protestations of virtue may have been they were not entirely convincing. The public was not satisfied. The Bureau of Corporations was established in 1903 and began investigations of the Standard Oil, American Tobacco Company and other trusts. In 1904 the Supreme Court of the United States declared the Northern Securities Company a combination in restraint of trade. In 1911 the Standard Oil Company and the American Tobacco were dissolved into constituent companies. In these prosecutions there still seemed to be a feeling that self-help should be encouraged and private initiative should prevail, but only under competitive conditions. It soon became apparent that the dissolution suits had not accomplished their purpose since the constituent companies were still largely controlled by the individuals who formerly controlled the trusts.

In 1914 the Federal Trade Commission was established and was empowered to investigate trade practices and issue "cease and desist" orders against those practices which seemed to involve "unfair" competition. In the same year the Clayton Act was passed and there was an attempt to specify certain acts considered to be illegal. It was declared that price discriminations in connection with interstate commerce were unlawful under certain conditions. Exclusive selling or leasing contracts, acquisition of stock in one corporation by another, interlocking directorates under certain conditions, were declared to be unlawful. This legislation seemed to recognize that it was difficult, if not impossible, to enforce pre-monopolistic conditions. It also seemed to suggest that the practice of self-reliance, honesty and industry had little meaning apart from the observance of specific trade practices or rather avoidance of certain condemned practices. Virtue was to be defined and made concrete.

The legislation did not attain the results expected from it. The loop-hole was that these practices were unlawful only when they tended substantially to lessen competition or tended to create a monopoly. This was less easy to show than had been expected. Effective prohibition of such practices did not occur.[14]

The business men themselves, because of the efforts to control certain practices and because of the greater development in industrial technique which turned out goods in such volume that attention to sales became imperative, attempted to enforce certain practices which they regarded as virtuous economic behavior. This was mainly attempted through Trade Associations or "co-operative competition," as it was sometimes called. These associations grew rapidly during and immediately following the World War.[15] Statistical and technical research bureaus were established. Attention was given to "Public Relations," employer-employee relations, credit and commercial research, and cost-accounting systems, among other activities. There was some defection from the policies of the associations by various members. Some members seemed to think that the trade association was an agency through which one could obtain information concerning a competitor's business. But in other cases the trade associations seem to have been fairly successful in maintaining the observance of certain practices.

The trade associations were and still are particularly vociferous in their demands for price maintenance. Some of the associations feel that price cutting is a great economic vice. The virtuous man is one who does not cut prices. An article in The American Machinist for March 22, 1928, p. 493, stated:

There are some manufacturers who have the courage to establish prices and maintain them. Their price is their price and they refuse to dicker. But there are some who lack the courage and the strength. And just so there are some purchasing agents who do not haggle. They ask for bids from suppliers whose product is acceptable and the low man gets the business. But there are others who seem to consider their function one of dollar squeezing; and the length to which this gentle art is carried is astonishing. . . .

After all, it gets down to a very simple consideration of plain honesty. If a purchasing agent lies or otherwise deceives a bidder into cutting his price, he is not dealing honestly. He is not fair. And if a manufacturer offers a bid that is not fair, either because the goods are not worth the money, or because he has padded the price for trading purposes, he is not dealing honestly. It is not square when you come down to the plain facts. It is trickery. It is an effort to take advantage of the other fellow.

Perhaps the trade associations have been successful in maintaining prices. The Hoover Committee on Recent Economic Changes reports that the period 1922 to 1928 was characterized by a considerable degree of price stability.[16] How much of the price stability during that period was due to the efforts of trade associations to enforce a certain type of conduct is not known. At any rate the efforts at price maintenance illustrate an attempt on the part of some business men to define virtuous economic behavior in terms of specific types of conduct rather than by reference to ambiguous words such as self-help, industry, and honesty.

Some different interpretations of the economic virtues are apparent, at least in the statements, if not the conduct, of individual outstanding business men. After the war there was something of a feeling on the part of business men that the public should be made to feel that the businesses were peculiarly interested in the public's welfare and needs. This was partly to increase customers and partly to forestall demands for investigation and public regulation of various enterprises. Of course business men had previously asserted that their main concern in life was with the "public welfare." But the type of conduct preached became somewhat different from the traditional formula regarding economic virtues. John D. Rockefeller, Jr., feels that the amassing of wealth is not sufficient justification for business activity. He says:

Men are coming to see that human life is of infinitely greater value than material wealth; that the health, happiness and well-being of the individual, however humble, is not to be sacrificed to the selfish aggrandizement of the more fortunate or powerful. Modern thought is placing less emphasis on material considerations. It is recognizing that the basis of national progress, whether industrial or social, is the health, efficiency, and spiritual development of the people.[17]

Aside from his gifts to colleges, universities, hospitals, clinics, research bureaus and churches he has interested himself in workers' representation in industry. After a serious strike in the Colorado Fuel and Iron Company in 1913-14 he introduced a plan under which employees, by secret ballot, elect representatives who act on their behalf in matters concerning sanitation, recreation, education, wages and employment.

The conduct of controllers of corporations has also attracted his attention. In March, 1929, Rockefeller succeeded in gathering enough proxies to oust Col. R. W. Stewart from the management of the Standard Oil Company of Indiana on the ground that Stewart's conduct did not represent the highest business standards.

Edward A. Filene of Boston is another business man whose ideas of proper business conduct vary somewhat from the traditional norm. He says, "The business of the future cannot be commercially successful unless it is socially sound."

The successful businesses of the future will be those that improve the processes and reduce the costs of production, rid distribution of its present indefensible wastes, bring the prices of necessities of life lower and lower, shorten hours of labor and enlarge the margin of leisure, eliminate periodic depression and recurrent unemployment and limit the area of the industrial battlefield.[18]

Mr. Owen D. Young, chairman of the Board of the General Electric Company, sees managers of corporations as trustees of the public welfare.

We think of managers no longer as the partisan attorneys of either group against the other. Rather we have come to consider them trustees of the whole undertaking, whose responsibility is to see to it on the one side that the invested capital is safe and that its return is adequate and continuous; and on the other side that competent and conscientious men are found to do the work and that their job is safe and their earnings are adequate and continuous.[19]

Many others, such as the late Mr. Mitten of the street railways in Philadelphia, Henry S. Dennison, Dwight Morrow, and Henry Ford, could be mentioned as examples of business leaders who believe that the private pursuit of money-making should not be the sole activity of those connected with the management of business.

These sentiments are mentioned for what they are worth. Whether they are practiced or not the sentiments at least reflect the feeling on the part of some money-makers that their activities should be defended in terms different from those used by the money-makers in the oil and steel industries at an earlier date.

Are these sentiments typical of all the more recent "leaders" in business enterprise? Consider the situation in some of the newer industries such as automobiles, electrical equipment, electrical utilities, radio, and moving pictures. In some of these industries, if not all, corporate structures have been developed in a manner which makes possible a great deal of private money-making, and relieves the insiders of any great responsibility for their acts.

The control of wealth by corporations is very extensive. In 1920 about 22 per cent of the entire industrial wealth of the country was concentrated in some two hundred managements.[20] The extensiveness of this control may be best illustrated by an actual example of a few of these intercorporate relationships. The General Electric Company is connected with the Radio Corporation of America and the Radio Corporation is tied up with the Westinghouse Electric Company. The General Electric Company also controls The Electric Bond and Share Company, a holding company which controls the American and Foreign Power Company. This company controls the public utilities of eleven foreign countries and has large holdings in six other countries. Within the United States the Electric Bond and Share directly controls companies in twenty-nine States producing fifteen per cent of the power used in the United States. Nor is this all. The General Electric Company has acquired sixty per cent of the stock (non-voting) of the General Electric Company of Great Britain and has acquired approximately one-third interest in the German General Electric Company.[21] And interlocking directorates probably bring these companies into close working arrangements with many other concerns in this country and in foreign countries.

These interrelationships create a favorable opportunity for large profits. The holding company device may enable a relatively small investment in the top holding company to control a much larger investment in the subsidiary operating companies. The Federal Trade Commission refers to one case in which an investment of a banking company of less than $1,000,000 in the top holding company of a pyramid of holding companies effectively controlled more than $370,000,000 of operating capital.[22] Because the reports of some of the holding companies are so meager it is impossible to state how much money is made by transactions with the controlled companies. It was reported to the Federal Trade Commission that the total earnings of the Electric Bond and Share Company for 1927 was $18,513,299.85. The earnings from commissions and supervision fees ("services" rendered to the controlled companies) accounted for $9,373,-172.07 of the total.[23]

In one of the companies controlled by the Insull group "the chief controlling company received $4,252,000 or nearly one third of the $13,982,000 of its subsidiaries' income, whereas it furnished only about $66,000,000 or a little more than one sixth of the total investment of $353,000,000."[24] It would seem that gratifyingly large profits revert to those in control of the controlling company. Nor is it difficult for this control to be maintained in a way that will insure profits. Most corporation acts to-day permit the incorporators to set out such powers as they care to have. By means of a number of devices the ordinary shareholders may find that their rights rapidly disappear. Additional stock may be issued; the stock may be no-par and issued at a lower figure than preceding issues, thus decreasing the value of outstanding shares; the shareholders may not be permitted to purchase additional stock; dividends may be withheld; blank stock may be issued to be filled in at a later time. Through these devices the controllers of the corporation may shift the earnings from the general body of shareholders to themselves.[25]

Do the gentlemen connected with the control of these companies manifest any of the economic virtues, either traditional or new? The question may best be answered by a glance at one or two individuals that seem to be representative money makers in the newer industries and have made money under the new conditions.

Samuel J. Insull is a conspicuous leader in the field of electrical utilities. Insull started his career in London as an office boy at $1.25 a week. He learned shorthand and answered an advertisement in a London newspaper asking for a secretary to work from eleven to three.[26] It happened that the man who advertised for a secretary was Thomas A. Edison's London agent. Insull obtained the job and through his employer learned something of the telephone business. And in his position he carried on some correspondence with Edison. Shortly afterward Edison himself needed a secretary and wrote to his London agent for suggestions. The London agent recommended Insull and Edison offered Insull the job. This was in 1881 when Insull was twenty-one years old.[27]

When a group of New York bankers offered to back Edison in the manufacture and sale of electric lamps Insull got into the organization as Edison's business representative. In 1889 he was made vice-president of the Edison General Electric Company. When this company was consolidated with the Thomas-Huston Electric interests in 1892, Insull became vice-president of the new company, The General Electric Company.[28]

His financial position was becoming sufficiently strong to permit his branching out for himself. He resigned his position in the General Electric Company and became president of the Chicago Edison Company and the Commonwealth Electric Company. And in 1907 these two companies were consolidated into the Commonwealth Edison Company in which Insull attained control.

This did not end his money-making activities. He continued to consolidate operating companies and control them through holding companies. Instead of merely consolidating isolated operating companies he and his associates developed territorial consolidations. Holding companies were established to control operating companies throughout a large territory. The main holding companies were: The Middle West Utilities Company, The Central and Southwest Utilities Company, The Northwest Utilities Company, and the New England Public Service Company. The names suggest the territory controlled. The companies controlled by Insull served 1,836 communities at the end of 1925. Since that time the control has been extended.

As was pointed out before, these consolidations and controls are significant because they greatly increase opportunities for money making. A relatively small investment in the top holding company controls the revenue derived from very large investments in the operating companies. The investments in the operating companies are expected to come from the general public investor. The owners of about one-third of the stock of the Middle Western Utilities Company control a total investment of fifty-three million dollars. The book value of the stock of the Middle Western is twenty-eight millions.[29] In another Insull company, the American Public Utilities Company, thirty per cent of the total capital securities carries with it control and receives about four-ninths of the income accruing to voting stocks after prior preferred stocks. It has already been mentioned that the Middle Western company receives about one-third of its subsidiaries' net income and contributes about one-sixth of the total investment.

Holding companies, even though they may be connected with

public utility operating companies are not subject to public regulation. And with the newer strategy of corporation finance few
restraints are put on individual enterprise. Having briefly considered Insull's activity it may be interesting to turn to his ideas
of economic virtues.

Insull seems to revere the traditional virtues of self-help,
industry, and honesty. He says he got his start in business from
reading Samuel Smiles's Self Help.[30] He also thinks that one
can get to the top by ambition, courage, and hard work.[31] He
says private enterprise should not be discouraged by extending
and amplifying the public regulation of utilities. This would be
bad for society, he feels, since it would "check enterprise and
individuality in management."[32]

In short, Insull adheres to the traditional formula for economic virtues that was preached by the money-makers of an
earlier day. He does mention other activities which he feels
represent virtuous economic behavior. One should not go into
business to make money, but to be a great leader. "Money-making is incidental to leadership."[33] And a great leader is really a
public servant. Of course utilities usually talk a great deal of
service. In March, 1928, the Saint Francis Dam in California
burst. Generating stations in Los Angeles were incapacitated.
The electrical needs of Los Angeles were temporarily supplied by
the Southern California Edison Company. An editorial in The
Electrical World commented on the event, "Chairman Miller,
President Ballard and the entire Edison organization are so
rooted and grounded in traditions of service that if human im-
pulses and the needs of California did not stir them, their natural
instinct for service would."[34]

Perhaps Insull also believes in a "natural instinct for service." At least he has talked so much about service that Samuel
Crowthers has called him "The Public's Hired Man." Insull is
thought to be encouraging community ownership of public utilities, that is, the public is encouraged to invest in his companies.[35]
But no virtues are preached which interfere with money-making.

The utilities urge their employees to emphasize service and
keep in touch with the public. The National Electric Light Asso-

ciation formulated the conduct recommended to people in the
utility field. The conduct they considered virtuous was:

Boundless energy. Infinite tact. Absolute accuracy. Initiative. Self-reliance and reliability. Enthusiasm which will not be
downed. Address and ability to hold his own on the public plat-
form. Industry. Popularity which will counteract the prejudice
against such men as the collector of taxes and other monthly levies
such as gas and electric light bills. Intimate knowledge of municipal affairs and of the shameful waste of municipal operation.[36]

Apparently some of the conduct is recommended to forestall
any further public regulation or public operation of public utilities.

In 1926 Insull seemed to fear that public statements about
service were not entirely convincing to office holders who might
have something to say about regulation of utilities. He tried to
make the argument more convincing by giving $15,000 to the
campaign fund of G. P. Brennan, Democratic candidate for
Senator from Illinois. He then contributed $125,000 to the cam-
paign fund of Frank L. Smith, Republican candidate for the same
office.[37]

John J. Raskob is one of the millionaires created by the auto-
mobile industry and the stock market. Until recently he was
chairman of the Finance Committee of the General Motors Company. He is sometimes referred to as a self-made man. He
started as a stenographer at five dollars a week.[38] He wrote to an
old friend who had gone to Ohio asking if there were any jobs
in that vicinity. The friend replied that Pierre S. Du Pont, in
Lorain, Ohio, was looking for a secretary. Raskob applied and
received a position as secretary at one thousand dollars a year.
Raskob was then twenty-one years old. Du Pont liked the secretary and when Du Pont became treasurer of the E. I. Du Pont de
Nemours Company in Wilmington, Del., he took Raskob with
him and made him assistant treasurer. Raskob persuaded Du
Pont to assist him in the purchase of General Motors stock. They
secured some three thousand shares. This was in 1913. Some
bankers had a five-year voting trust of the common stock which
was to terminate in October, 1915. The bankers wanted to continue the voting trust. W. C. Durant wanted to terminate the

voting trust and gain control of General Motors. The bankers and Durant competed so vigorously for the control that each party had practically an equal amount of stock. The result was that Du Pont and Raskob, with their three thousand shares, were in a strong strategic position. A compromise was reached. The bankers and Durant were each allowed to nominate seven directors and Du Pont was permitted to nominate three directors. Raskob and Du Pont became directors of the General Motors Company.[39] Although Raskob did not have control of the company he was on the inside. He persuaded the Du Pont Company to invest $50,000,000. By the beginning of 1929 this investment had increased in value to $600,000,000.[40]

Raskob was very active in the stock market.

Through him more clearly than most industrial leaders it is possible to discern the enormous opportunities for stock market profits that were open to men in charge of great corporations during the long bull market. The market in its final phases was, like professional baseball, largely made possible by newspaper publicity, some alleged newspapers even going so far as to tout daily tips.[41]

Other individuals became prominent stock market speculators during the 1922-1929 bull market and amassed large fortunes. Such individuals as Durant, Jesse L. Livermore, Arthur W. Cutten, Frank E. Bliss, Benjamin Block, Michael J. Meehan, Joseph E. Higgins, the Fisher Brothers from Detroit, Louis W. Zimmerman are some of those who have been called the new "Mystery Men of Wall Street."[42]

The economic virtues that were recommended for others were thrift and investment. As Raskob states the case:

It is a great principle of industrial success to-day that principle of making brains and brawn a part owner of your business, and thereby getting them to put all of their energy and intelligence and loyalty into the job. We help our laboring men to save and to invest in General Motors and we have no labor troubles.[43]

Economic virtues for the business enterprises during the twentieth century have received new formulation in some lines of business, but not all. In the face of supposedly hostile legislation and changed conditions of business activity some groups tried to define virtuous behavior in terms of specific trade practices. Other business men did not emphasize money-making in itself nor private initiative, but attempted to tell just what they were doing as business leaders for the improvement of economic conditions.

The individuals connected with the newer industries carried self-help to the higher realms of corporation finance and speculation. Their statements regarding economic virtues should perhaps be interpreted as lip service to that conduct which they thought the public would applaud.

Let us see what has happened to the homely virtue of thrift during this period.

FOOTNOTES FOR CHAPTER VII

[1] M. W. Watkins, *Industrial Combinations and Public Policy*, Appendix 2 and chs. 2, 3.

[2] J. A. Ryan, *A Living Wage*.

[3] *U. S. Census of Manufactures*. Part IV, pp. 645, 648.

[4] Scott Nearing, *Social Adjustment*, ch. 4.

[5] F. H. Streightoff, *The Standard of Living*, p. 244. On the condition of the worker in the new regime see T. Veblen, *The Theory of Business Enterprise*, ch. 8; *The Vested Interests and the State of the Industrial Arts*, ch. 2.

[6] Mark Sullivan, *Our Times*. Vol. 2, pp. 311-313.

[7] *Political Science Quarterly*. Vol. XXIV, pp. 283-306, article on "Unfair Competition," by W. S. Stevens. Also pp. 460-490. Also M. W. Watkins, *op. cit.*, ch. 5.

[8] *McClure's Magazine*. Vol. 22, pp. 323ff., "The Right to Work," and pp. 366ff., "A Corner in Labor."

[9] *Independent Magazine*, May 1, 1902, pp. 1027ff., "The Concentration of Wealth," a symposium. See Russell Sage, p. 1027, and J. J. Hill, to the same effect, p. 1029.

[10] *The Cosmopolitan*. Vol. 45, 1908, p. 479.

[11] *The Cosmopolitan*, 1902, p. 292.

[12] *Banker's Magazine*. Vol. 86, p. 180.

[13] U. S. Industrial Commission, *Report*. 1901. Vol. 13, p. 461.

[14] H. R. Seager and C. A. Gulick, Jr., *Trust and Corporation Problems*, 1929, pp. 453ff.

[15] *Ibid.*, p. 306.

[16] *Recent Economic Changes*, pp. xiii and xiv.

[17] J. D. Rockefeller, Jr., *Representation in Industry*, p. 28.

[18] Quoted in *New York World*, May 14, 1928.

[19] *Bulletin of the International Management Institute*, Vol. 2, No. 2, February, 1928.

[20] *American Economic Review*, March, 1930, A. A. Berle, Jr., and G. C. Means, "Corporations and The Public Investor."

[21] L. Denny, *America Conquers Britain*, pp. 139-149.

[22] Quoted in W. E. Mosher and others, *Electrical Utilities*, p. 95.

[23] *Ibid.*, p. 106.

[24] Federal Trade Commission, *Control of Power Companies—Electric Power Industry*, 1927, p. 259.

[25] See footnote 20 above.

[26] Samuel Insull, *Public Utilities in Modern Life*, pp. 186, 191.

[27] *Ibid.*, p. 191.

[28] Federal Trade Commission, *op. cit.* ch. 23 on the Insull group of utilities.

[29] *Ibid.*, p. 258.

[30] Samuel Insull, *op. cit.* p. 137.

[31] *Ibid.*, p. 136.

[32] *Ibid.*, p. 31.

[33] *Ibid.*, p. 39.

[34] *Electrical World*, March 24, 1928, The San Franscisquito Disaster.

[35] *Collier's Weekly*, January 17, 1925, Samuel Insull, by Samuel Crowthers.

[36] Samuel Insull, *op. cit.* pp. 328-329.

[37] As reported in *The Literary Digest*, August 14, 1926, p. 10.

[38] *The New York World*, July 12, 1928.

[39] Earl Sparling, *Mystery Men of Wall Street*, New York, 1930, p. 210.

[40] *Ibid.*, p. 213.

[41] *Ibid.*, pp. 206-207.

[42] *Ibid.*, passim.

[43] *The New York World*, July 12, 1928.

CHAPTER VIII

SAVING AND SPENDING

THE advocacy of thrift on the one hand and greater immediate spending on the other illustrates the manner in which various groups found it to their economic advantage to advocate virtue. The conflict between thrift and spending also further illustrates the influence of changing economic conditions on ideas concerning virtuous economic behavior.

Banking institutions, particularly savings banks, were anxious to see the traditional economic virtues prevail. They were particularly interested in thrift, which to them was a matter of savings deposits. They argued that such thrift was of great benefit to society. A writer in the Bankers' Magazine in September, 1908, said:

> The institution that . . . tends to foster the spirit of thrift performs a number of closely connected services to the community. It not only benefits the man and his family, by making them all better dressed and better fed and better housed, and better fitted to look into the future, but it helps in the general good. The working capital is greater, the producing capacity is enlarged, and the wealth of the nation is increased by every dollar that the thrifty man places in the savings bank.[1]

The bankers were not, of course, purely disinterested in their advocacy of thrift. Society was not alone in receiving the rewards of virtue. As one banker put the matter:

> Not the least of the many thrift-day advantages is the opportunity afforded the banker of acquainting the public with his ideals of service. . . . The banker is . . . brought directly before the public in an attractive rôle in a new light. He is humanized in the popular eye and shown to be highly approachable —a fact mutually advantageous.
>
> To trust companies thrift day brings additional advantages. The thrifty man keeps a healthy balance in his checking account. The thrifty man . . . appreciates the necessity of making a

will and the advantages of securing the service of a trust company in an executive and administrative capacity.[2]

Thrift, interpreted as monetary deposits in banks, took on new life as a result of the bankers' efforts to increase their business. A campaign was started and, first of all, the great lack of thrift was indicated. There was a general feeling that the Americans had been quite wasteful in their use of natural resources and that they had failed to provide carefully for the future.[3] The bankers went on to point out that the per cent of savers in the total population in America was only 18 per cent, while in France about 34 per cent of the total population were savers.[4] They also asserted:

It is a well-known fact that Americans individually earn more money than citizens of any other nation in the world, and at the same time are the greatest spenders. Out of one hundred million people there are registered in this country only approximately fifteen million savings accounts. . . .

With the right kind of a nation-wide movement for individual thrift it is quite possible to foresee that twenty-five, or even fifty persons, out of each one hundred of the population can be registered on the books of the financial institutions of the United States.[5]

This last statement was a call for more vigor in pushing the campaign. The campaign had been launched some two years before, in 1914. The American Society for Thrift had been organized and held its first meeting on January 13, 1914. Mr. S. W. Straus was elected president. In 1915 an International Congress for Thrift was held at the Panama-Pacific Exposition in San Francisco. In August, 1915, the Board of Directors of the National Education Association approved the suggestion that a committee be appointed to be known as the Committee on Thrift Education.[6]

Articles in the Bankers' Magazine had already pointed out the lack of thrift education and had applauded the passing of a law in Massachusetts which made thrift instruction in the public schools compulsory.[7] The schools generally throughout the country vigorously inculcated thrift. Since there was a feeling that education must be somehow uplifting and since morality in America has devoted much effort to recommending the economic virtues, the schools, through the National Education Association, sprang to their task with avidity. The campaign continued after the war and the National Education Association reported much progress. School children were encouraged to start thrift accounts, textbooks on thrift were issued and the savings banks were profitably pleased by the great increase of virtue among the younger generation.[8]

Further alliances were made between the bankers and groups which had the welfare of the country at heart. The Woman's Christian Temperance Union, the Y. M. C. A., the Y. W. C. A. and the churches thought thrift should be encouraged. Since ministers sometimes are puzzled over material for sermons, the bankers thoughtfully gave them suggestions. They said:

In view of the fact that the clergy all over the land are taking an intense interest in the thrift movement, and are everywhere preaching thrift from the pulpit, there is also furnished . . . a booklet containing suggestions for sermons.[9]

With such affiliations the bankers became optimistic. They said:

Business and professional men are always willing to cooperate in a movement which aims to promote the welfare of the community, and when these men work together through organization with the local clergy, the school principals and teachers, the officers of the Y. M. C. A., and other organizations, a mighty force is at work. All the strength, intelligence and good citizenship of the community are united in a common cause, and cannot fail to be successful.[10]

Despite the bankers' optimism the campaign met some opposition. As was pointed out at the beginning of the chapter the wage-earners in America were hardly in a position to lay aside and save their earnings, however admirable such activity might be. Some observers made light of the necessity to save and recited hypothetical cases of individuals who had saved, denied themselves pleasures, only to be left with an inheritance in later years.[11] Others pointed out that business was developing sales

organizations and pleading with the consumer to spend his dollars. Such practices were discouraging the laying aside of money
for some future contingency.[12] And one economist, Simon N.
Patten, became so bold as to say, thrift is no longer an economic
virtue. "The non-saver," he said, "is now a higher type of man
than the saver. . . . This higher family aims to create a flow
of income to enjoy and not an accumulating fund for future
support."[13] His article was the occasion for many feature articles
in the Sunday supplements of newspapers which pointed out the
errors in his statements.

The critics were answered. As for those who said that freer
spending was encouraged by business practices and was necessary
if business were to continue at a profitable level, they misunder-
stood the economic process. In an article entitled "The Thrift
Campaign versus 'Business as Usual,'" C. C. Arbuthnot, Professor of Economics at Western Reserve University, claimed that
such curtailment of purchases as resulted from bank deposits did
not create business depression. In fact, such savings might
increase prosperity since they could be invested in industry
and lead to greater employment and a greater distribution of
wages.[14]

Before this discussion could be settled the World War had
started. Considered from the standpoint of all nations involved
there was much destruction of lives, property and savings. In
America the war became an occasion for the further appeal for
individual thrift.

Thrift became patriotic. The president of the Thrift Association, speaking before the National Council of Education in
1918, said:

America to-day stands in the position in which all her economic problems must be solved through thrift. Whether we consider plans for the successful defeat of those sinister forces that
are pounding at the very foundations of civilization, or whether
we have in mind the smallest details of home and business routine,
the answer remains the same. And unless America can learn the
full and solemn truth of these facts, unless our people gain a
deep, sincere appreciation of the absolute necessity for thrift, we
cannot hope to hold the proud position we occupy as the flag-

bearer of nations—the leader in the fight for the lofty ideals of human betterment.[15]

Others who were interested in the Thrift Campaign quickly pointed out the relation between thrift and patriotism.[16] Sugarless days, wheatless days, meatless days, gasolineless days, cultivation of war gardens, increase of savings deposits, the purchase of war-savings stamps and Liberty Bonds, all these were taken as evidence of the increase of thrift and economy that resulted from the war. It was also stated that by becoming patriotic individuals became thrifty. It was even suggested that if the World War accomplished nothing else, it had performed a great service in encouraging thrift. Like France, America would be characterized by a large number of small investors. These people would feel they had a stake in the country and the major part of labor troubles would be solved.[17]

It seems strange that war should be considered an incentive to thrift. While individual savings deposits increased, the mobilization of materials for the prosecution of the war was accompanied by great extravagance. As the Beards observed:

Under the cost-plus system no one was interested in economy; if the producer of raw materials raised his prices, the war contractor could smile and pass on the extra charge with an increase on his commission. If a trade union struck for higher wages, the manufacturer could grant the demand with a friendly shrug, for the additional expense meant a larger commission garnered from the beneficent government. . . . So the war led by a Democratic President strengthened his opposition by making several thousand millionaires in the course of two years and by pouring out billions in extra dividends frequently in the form of stock, thereby avoiding the taxes on income and profits. Even the staunchest patriots could hardly restrain their emotions as they contemplated the possibilities of the economic scene.[18]

The statements made by thrift advocates that the Liberty Loans were made possible by individual savings ignored the process by which these loans were taken up. "The truth is that a very considerable percentage of the funds raised for war uses did not come from individual savings, but were created by the banking institutions through a process of expanding the ratio of deposits to cash resources." At the time a Liberty Loan was being floated a bank might have one hundred thousand dollars of commercial paper available for rediscount. When this was rediscounted at the Federal Reserve bank a deposit of that amount less the discount was received in return. The bank was then in a position to extend the volume of its business since the deposit account constituted an increase in the lawful reserve of the bank. Something over seven hundred thousand dollars could then be invested in Liberty Bonds. This purchase was made possible by "the simple process of rediscounting the commercial notes of customers with the Federal Reserve bank, . . . the wherewithal being simply manufactured for the purpose."[19]

In 1918, the year in which thrift and individual savings were being most actively preached and advocated, the savings of the nation as a whole fell off tremendously, due, of course, to the war. In a rough estimate of "social savings," Dr. W. I. King arrived at the following figures:

SOCIAL SAVINGS

Calendar Year	Millions of dollars having a value equivalent to that of 1913
1913	4,880
1914	4,140
1915	7,381
1916	11,401
1917	7,162
1918	—1,196

King means by social savings an increase of net assets. The possibilities of divergence between this and individual savings are obvious. For example, a man is accustomed to putting $500 per annum into the savings bank. His home, worth $12,000, is destroyed. He buys another for $10,000. He increases his savings to pay for it. But while his savings are increasing, $2,000 worth of property has disappeared. The way in which King arrives at his figures is to discover the increase over a period of years of such things as acreage of crops, live stock, gold coin, railroad equipment, property rights in foreign countries, etc.[20]

In the years following the war the thrift campaign met re-
newed opposition. Business men with goods to sell thought the
volume of sales would diminish if too much emphasis was put on
thrift and savings. The depression of 1921 was interpreted as a
"buyers' strike." If prosperity was to be regained then sales
resistance should be broken down and people should not be encouraged to lay aside their money for some future time. The
National Prosperity Bureau addressed the Benjamin Franklin
Memorial Committee of the New York Thrift Commission as
follows:

> The mere word "thrift," variously defined by thrift expo-
> nents to meet their respective objects, means in practice, if it
> means anything, to buy less. How can buying less open up closed
> mills and halt failures? We are opposed to any sort of thrift
> which leads to industrial stagnation. We are against any new
> national thrift policy which creates a financial imperialism. We
> repudiate a thrift, no matter how alluring its guise, which inevi-
> tably reduces the living standards of American workingmen to
> the niggardly requisites of certain immigrants.[21]

So loudly did the business men proclaim the virtues of spending
instead of saving that they convinced themselves that the depression of 1921 was overcome by their phenomenal sales efforts.[22]

There were very good reasons for this outburst. It was the
acknowledgment of an economic development that had been going
on for some time. Through the development of larger units of
business, through the greater application of science to technical
processes and machine production the productive capacity of the
country was greatly increased. It seemed that more goods could
be produced than could ever be sold at a profit if this productive
capacity were allowed to turn the goods out. Furthermore the
process of curtailing production was not so easy as it had been
once. The machinery represented heavy investments and if the
machinery were permitted to lie idle it deteriorated rapidly
through disuse. In many cases it was cheaper to keep the machinery running than to stop it entirely. Even though goods
were sold below cost some return would be realized for payment
of overhead costs. Consequently more and more emphasis was

put on volume of sales. As each business enterprise or industry attempted to reduce its own overhead costs greater emphasis was put on beating the competitor to the market. Sales competition increased and greater pressure was exerted to force the consumer to spend his dollar.[23] In this situation it is not surprising that these business men should consider greater spending an economic virtue.

Henry Ford lent the weight of his influence to this tendency. But before the consumer can spend he must have sufficient purchasing power. He explains how this should work toward prosperity. He says:

The real progress of our company dates from 1914, when we raised the minimum wage from somewhat more than two dollars a day to a flat five dollars a day, for then we increased the buying power of our own people, and they increased the buying power of other people, and so on and on. It is this thought of enlarging buying power by paying high wages and selling at low prices which is behind the prosperity of this country.[24]

But if this policy is to be successful, then people must be encouraged to spend instead of save. Some saving would remain but the emphasis would be placed on immediate spending. Ford recommends spending not merely because of its beneficent effect on economic development but because it helps the individual get ahead. He says:

No successful boy ever saved any money. They spent it just as fast as they could for things to improve themselves. . . . It is time enough to save when you can earn more than you can spend wisely. But you will never get to that point by saving.

The economic virtue which Ford considers more important than saving is industry. By working hard the individual can increase his income and then have more money to invest in himself, which eventually means greater opportunity for success.[25]

Installment selling, as a device to increase sales, was another factor leading to less emphasis on saving and more emphasis on immediate spending. According to one estimate installment sales at the end of 1926 amounted to about four and one-half billion dollars out of a total retail sale of about thirty-eight billions. But the practice seemed to be growing.[26] Possible objections, from those who might fear installment selling would decrease saving, were anticipated.

> To the extent that the installment purchase of a durable commodity which is worth having stimulates the possessor to renewed and increased exertion, it acts as an encouragement, and not as a discouragement, to savings.[27]

However, the general influence of installment selling seemed to be in the direction of buying more immediately instead of waiting until one had laid aside enough money to completely pay for the commodity.

The campaign against thrift and saving was aided by a theory of the business cycle which emphasized thrift as one of the factors causing business depression. The writings of W. T. Foster and W. Catchings gave currency to the view that saving was an economic vice rather than an economic virtue. They say:

> The thrifty individual, it is true, has saved five dollars, and is very likely better off for his thrift. What are savings for an individual, however, are not necessarily savings for society. Everyone who saves money at times when his abstinence helps to curtail production and throw men out of work saves at the expense of other people. For the individual, a penny saved is a penny earned; but for society a penny saved is sometimes a penny lost.[28]

According to their analysis a mere increase of spending is not possible unless there is sufficient money disbursed to buy the goods that are produced. A greater disbursement of incomes would be useless unless they were spent instead of being saved.

Despite this attack on the ancient virtue of thrift the bankers still insisted that thrift should be increased and they continued to wage their campaign to persuade people to save.[29] There was some feeling that they were being successful.[30] Furthermore they were encouraged by a new alignment in the field of industry.

Corporations had been encouraging their employees to purchase stock in the companies for which they worked. The motives seemed to be to continue and encourage thrift, and to get a more loyal and efficient labor force.[31] This had been hailed as a revolutionary development in American economic life. It was to "wipe out the distinction between laborers and capitalists." This could only be accomplished by more thrift. Encouragement should be given to the growth of savings deposits, the growth of labor banks, and to the investment by laborers in shares of corporations.[32]

The wage earner is thus put in the perplexing position of being urged to spend his income on the one hand and to save money to invest on the other.

It may be interesting to inquire as to the amount of income large sections of the populace receive and the possibilities provided by these incomes for the practice of thrift and saving. According to a study by the National Bureau of Economic Research the statistics of income for 1918 reveal that about 86 per cent of persons who were gainfully employed had incomes of less than $2,000, and about 14 per cent had incomes exceeding that amount.[33] In a later study by the same research bureau the average annual income per employee, by industry groups, in the United States for 1925 was as follows:[34]

	Average income per employee
1. Agriculture	$537
2. Mining	1,318
3. Manufacturing	1,362
4. Construction	1,574
5. Transportation and public utilities	1,554
6. Banking	2,179
7. Merchandising	1,315
8. Government	1,585
9. Unclassified industries	1,408
10. Miscellaneous income	....
11. All groups combined	1,384

In 1925 Paul Douglas estimated that between $2,000 and $2,400 was necessary in the larger cities for the maintenance of a "minimum-of-comfort" level of living, a level which would make possible savings and insurance against industrial risks. As the above figures would seem to indicate and as Douglas says, "Such a level of living . . . has been attained by only a small proportion of the industrial wage-earners."[35] If savings are made on such incomes it means a decrease in other items of the budget which are perhaps more necessary than savings. Furthermore workers past forty years of age are finding it increasingly difficult to find employment. Their own individual thrift could not be sufficient to provide for this permanent unemployment.[36]

Again, the rather rough estimate of national savings made by Dr. King would seem to indicate that, as would be expected, the workers are responsible for less of the total national savings than are other groups. Although numerically the workers represent the largest occupational group they contribute but twenty per cent of the total national savings; the agricultural interests contribute twelve per cent and business men and property owners contribute sixty-eight per cent of the total. This was for the period from 1909 to 1918.[37] The percentages may suggest too great an exactness in the estimate of savings. As a rough approximation the percentages indicate something of the proportion of savings made by different income groups. The relatively small amount of national savings attributable to wage-earners would seem to be due to lack of income rather than lack of the virtue of thrift. But the advocates of saving on the one hand and the advocates of immediate spending on the other did not base their campaigns on income statistics. It was the needs of their own business that convinced them of the virtue of such acts.

If one is to understand the history of economic virtues, particularly since the beginning of the century, it would seem to be necessary to consider the matter in terms of various economic groups who find it to their advantage to recommend one or another of the so-called economic virtues. Those who find it to their advantage to recommend savings are prone to think of this type of thrift as being a general economic virtue. On the other hand those who are anxious to stimulate sales are inclined to think of saving as an economic vice. For these people virtue consists in spending more. Since our economic life is so complex and as yet is so imperfectly understood these interested groups find little difficulty in discovering "scientific" analyses of economic conditions which support their respective positions. As for some of the institutions which are thought to "mould public opinion," such as the churches and schools, we have seen that they are inclined to the side which advocates "self-help" and thrift. Perhaps this phenomenon is best understood in terms of the traditions, mentioned previously, which these institutions have inherited. They do not always advocate the interests of economic groups but they are interested in morality. This frequently reduces itself to an advocacy of thrift, prudence, and industry revolving about "self-help."

FOOTNOTES FOR CHAPTER VIII

[1] *Banker's Magazine*, September, 1908. Vol. 77, p. 871.

[2] *Banker's Magazine*. Vol. 94, p. 73.

[3] *The Independent*, June, 1910, "The Thriftless Generation." Also, *Literary Digest*, Nov., 1913, "The Unthrifty American."

[4] *Banker's Magazine*. Vol. 86, p. 117.

[5] *Banker's Magazine*. Vol. 92, p. 24.

[6] S. W. Straus, *History of the Thrift Movement in America*, pp. 69, 103, 119.

[7] *Banker's Magazine*. Vol. 86, p. 572.

[8] See the reports of the National Education Association, 1918, pp. 589-592; 1924, pp. 338-340; 1925, pp. 188-190. Also, *Banker's Magazine*. Vol. 86, pp. 570-572.

[9] *Banker's Magazine*. Vol. 93, p. 50.

[10] *Banker's Magazine*. Vol. 93, p. 47.

[11] *Living Age*, Feb. 17, 1912, article on "Thrift."

[12] *Independent*, June 30, 1910, article on "The Discouragement of Thrift."

[13] *Current Opinion*. Vol. 54, p. 51, "Extravagance as a Virtue," by S. N. Patten.

[14] *Banker's Magazine*. Vol. 97, pp. 16-22, "The Thrift Campaign versus 'Business as Usual.'"

[15] Straus, *History of the Thrift Movement in America*, p. 187.

[16] *Journal of National Education Association*. Vol. 95, pp. 49-50. "Thrift—A Patriotic Necessity."

[17] *Banker's Magazine*. Vol. 97, pp. 38ff., "Thrift—One Economic By-Product of the World War."

[18] Beard, *The Rise of American Civilization*. Vol. 2, pp. 636-637.

[19] H. G. Moulton, *The Financial Organization of Society*, pp. 628-629.

[20] *Journal of the American Statistical Association*, Sept. 1922, pp. 305-323; Dec., 1922, pp. 458-470, "The Net Volume of Savings in the United States," by W. I. King.

[21] Quoted in *The Nation*, Feb. 16, 1921, "The Menace of Thrift."

[22] Paul Mazur, *American Prosperity, passim*.

[23] S. Chase and F. J. Schlink, *Your Money's Worth*, ch. 2.

[24] Ford and Crowthers, *Today and Tomorrow*.

[25] Quoted in *The Literary Digest*, Dec. 29, 1928, p. 10.

[26] E. R. A. Seligman, *The Economics of Installment Selling.* Vol. I.

[27] *Ibid.* Vol. I, p. 276-277.

[28] *Atlantic Monthly.* Vol. 137, p. 539, "The Dilemma of Thrift."

[29] *American Bankers' Association Bulletin,* July, 1927, "Thrift—No Dilemma."

[30] *Literary Digest.* Vol. 91, p. 86, "Is a Thrift Wave on the Way?" Also, Saturday Evening Post. Vol. 199, p. 27, "Selling Thrift."

[31] National Industrial Conference Board, *Employee Stock Purchase Plans in the United States,* p. 41.

[32] T. N. Carver, *The Present Economic Revolution in the United States.* Ch. I.

[33] National Bureau of Economic Research, *Income in the United States,* 1921. p. 146.

[34] National Bureau of Economic Research, *Recent Economic Changes.* Vol. 2, p. 777.

[35] P. H. Douglas, *Wages and the Family,* p. 6.

[36] A. Epstein, *The Challenge of the Aged,* pp. 14-58.

[37] W. I. King, *op. cit.*

CHAPTER IX

CONCLUSIONS

THE different economic groups which have been examined in the preceding pages obviously represent but a small sample of the entire economic life in the United States. Each of the various groups seemed to have its own peculiar interpretations of the economic virtues and if a larger number of groups were studied one might find an even greater variety of economic virtues. Recognizing the limitation of the samples studied some generalizations concerning economic virtues may be ventured.

Certain types of conduct are recommended by various groups and individuals because they are thought to lead to the general economic welfare of society. On closer examination the welfare of society reduces itself to the welfare of a particular group. The respective groups have their own interpretations of the virtues and then they recommend these virtues to everyone else regardless of the diversity of economic conditions under which people live. To be sure there has been a continuous tradition regarding economic virtues in the United States, that is, the same words, such as self-reliance, thrift, industry, honesty, etc., have been used by different groups in different situations. But the meaning put into these words has varied. For example, industry does not mean the same thing, nor does it produce the same result when interpreted by the pioneer farmers as it does when interpreted by the business men.

The pioneer farmers asserted, for the benefit of the speculators and storekeepers, that neighborliness, honesty, and industry were economic virtues and should be practiced. They seemed to mean that the speculator should cease his activities and settle down to the cultivation of the soil and that the storekeepers should stop forcing the farmer to "sell himself bare" in order to pay his debts at the store.

The business men in the towns thought the farmers lacked the virtue of industry. They interpreted industry as increased

efforts at producing a surplus. The business men wanted to
break down the self-sufficiency of the farmers and encourage
them to buy manufactured goods. It was thought industry would
accomplish this aim. Honesty for the merchants meant fulfillment of contracts and payment of debts. They were anxious to
see this virtue prevail in the farming communities. They interpreted self-help as individual activity in money-making. Much
of this consisted in maintaining and improving one's pecuniary
status even though it was at the expense of others.

It happened that the business men's virtues became more
prevalent than did those of the farmers. This was partly because
business activity spread more widely than did the activity which
characterized the early self-sufficient farming community. The
farmers lost their self-sufficiency and to some extent became
business men themselves. Another factor in the diffusion of the
virtues was religion. Puritan doctrines emphasized frugality and
industry. Puritanism was also reconciled with individual activity
and money-making which gave these activities a religious sanction they had not hitherto possessed. Furthermore the Puritan
influence became influential in the schools and taught a type of
morality that emphasized self-help, frugality, and industry. Puritanism and its interpretation of economic virtues also became
aligned with patriotism through the New Englanders' efforts to
make the rest of the country conform to their own peculiar ideas
of conduct.

With the spread of this particular interpretation of economic
virtues the virtues were read into the past and projected into the
future. The frontier has frequently been interpreted as a society
in which the economic virtues as interpreted by a later business
group were dearly cherished and widely practiced.

The pioneer is thought to have been developing a society
"where should dwell comfort and the higher things of life,
though they might not be for him. Here, also, were the pioneer's traits, individual activity, inventiveness, and competition
for the prizes of the rich province that awaited exploitation under
freedom and equality of opportunity."[1] Later groups who happen to be interested in keen competition and individual activity
are pleased with such interpretations. They feel individual

activity is justified because it develops the resources of the country and produces the "higher things of life." By practicing individual activity they are proceeding in the American tradition and continuing the good work started by the pioneers.

On the basis of the above study of the hunter and farmer pioneers individual activity and keen competition would not seem to have been conspicuous traits of behavior. To be sure such behavior existed. Individual work on one's own land was obviously necessary and competition existed even if it manifested itself in such activities as corn huskings. But individual activity was hampered and restrained by community needs. The scarcity of labor encouraged co-operative activity in the heavier work. To mind one's own business under the circumstances was not interpreted as virtuous conduct. As for competition for the prizes of the rich province this was of little importance until the prizes could be sold. The pioneers neglected those areas of the West that were most fertile and which a later generation has valued most highly. The pioneers were living in self-sufficient groups and they settled in close proximity to supplies of wood and water instead of settling on the more fertile plains. Whatever individual activity existed on the frontier is to be understood in terms of the relative isolation of the frontier groups, the scarcity of labor, the relative lack of specialization and the resulting co-operative activity.

Not only have certain interpretations of economic virtues been read into the past, the effects of certain virtues in the past have been extended into the present. Calvin Colton wrote in 1840,

> Ours is a country where men start from an humble origin . . . . and where they can attain to the most elevated positions or acquire a large amount of wealth, according to the pursuits they elect for themselves. No exclusive privileges of birth, no entailment of estates, no civil or political disqualifications stand in their path; but one has as good a chance as another, according to his talents, prudence, and personal exertions. This is a country of self-made men, than which there can be no better in any state of society.[2]

All of which may have been true when he wrote.

Through the influence of religion, school instruction, and the propaganda of various interested parties such attitudes were crystallized into national dogmas. As F. J. Grund remarked, "The moment a man is known to have acquired a little property by his own industry, he receives credit for ingenuity and persever- ance, and is trusted on account of these virtues."[8]

The virtues were divorced from concrete situations and at- tributed to all or nearly all who had started with relatively little wealth and attained great fortune. The money-makers whose fortunes increased with the industrial development following the Civil War were practicing self-help, thrift and industry under somewhat different conditions and with somewhat different results than was the case when business enterprises were smaller and the individual enterprise and the partnership more prevalent. Self- help was virtuous in the earlier situation because it was thought that the prosperity of the individual and the prosperity of his busi- ness were one and the same. Not only was the individual becom- ing independent but the business was developing and supplying the population with more goods. Furthermore competition was thought to be widely practiced so that each producer strove to improve his product and increase his sales. All this was thought to be for the welfare of society and hence such activities repre- sented the economic virtues.

But those conditions soon passed and under the corporate form of business organization private fortune and the fortunes of the business were not always synonymous. But little attention, at least for a time, was paid to the results of self-help under the new conditions. The practice that Grund observed continued. If a man were wealthy and thought to be industrious and thrifty he was considered economically virtuous regardless of the results of his conduct; in other words a fetish was made of certain economic virtues and little regard was paid to the results of such behavior under changed economic conditions.

It might even be said that the new rich were not practicing the traditional virtues, at least in the traditional meaning that had been attached to the virtues. When business was on a small scale self-help had a definite meaning. One could work for a year or two, lay aside part of his wages and branch out into business on a small scale. The millionaires did not become millionaires by such means. Apart from the matter of pure luck in making a fortune the successful money-makers got their start by reliance on others, that is, their start in the concerns that brought them fortune was made possible by financial assistance from others. If they had waited until they had sufficient money saved from their own labor they probably would not have got very far on the road to wealth. Such self-help as they practiced was in the direction of getting in touch with those who had openings into profitable ventures. They advocated the virtues as long as money-making was not hampered.

The widespread belief that economic virtues consisted in the practice of individual activity, industry and thrift benefited the higher income groups more than it did the lower income groups. Insistence on individual activity would greatly hamper the efforts of workers in forming unions, but it would not greatly hamper the money-making activities of the insiders in a large corporation. Thrift might be unnecessary for the higher income groups, but impossible for the lower income groups. As long as thrift is considered a general economic virtue then poverty is dismissed as merely the result of vice on the part of the poor.

But business men did not adhere strictly to a rigid interpretation of economic virtues. As business conditions changed and as business men's ideas of money-making under the new conditions changed new virtues began to be stressed. Those who were anxious to maintain a large volume of sales talked about thrift as an economic vice and spending as an economic virtue. Those who thought profits would be increased by maintaining prices recommended price maintenance as an economic virtue. They argued it would increase general economic stability. It was not obvious that other groups in society would benefit by this policy since price stability is frequently accompanied by great irregularity in production and employment.[4] But since the business men thought stable prices were good for business they seem to have concluded they were good for the whole of society.

Some of the changes in the virtues preached by the business men resulted from adverse criticisms of their activity and from attempts to control certain business practices. Such statements of the economic virtues as the late Judge Gary made apparently implied that it was necessary to convince the public and the government that business conduct had changed and therefore it would not be necessary for the government to interfere in the United States Steel Corporation. John D. Rockefeller, Jr., also seems to have become aware that certain business practices were being criticised. He, therefore, advocated certain conduct that he considered virtuous behavior for the new situation.

Such changes as have occurred in the traditional economic virtues are not sufficiently extensive to benefit all sections of the population. In the newer industries particularly, although there has been talk of "public service," private money-making by the insiders on the stock exchange or money-making at the expense of the general body of shareholders does not seem to have been severely restricted. In these realms financial success is attained in other ways than by a strict adherence to economic virtues, although the traditional virtues are used to defend such success as is attained by the more fortunate money-makers. Immediate spending instead of the ancient virtue of thrift is being advocated by some who feel this is a means of stimulating sales. This is partly due to the changed conditions under which business is carried on.

Of course, the appearance and dominance of some different group, such as the Soviet regime in Russia, would mean a radical change in economic virtues to be imposed on all members of the community. Or, without necessarily becoming dominant, certain groups, such as organized labor, public investors, or consumers, may become sufficiently articulate to see to it that their difficulties will be solved in terms of their own needs in specific situations rather than by appealing to traditional and ambiguous virtues.

FOOTNOTES FOR CHAPTER IX

[1] F. J. Turner, *The Frontier in American History*, p. 152.

[2] Quoted in C. R. Fish, *The Rise of the Common Man*, frontispiece.

[3] F. J. Grund, *The Americans*. Vol. 2, p. 9.

[4] H. R. Seager and C. A. Gulick, Jr. *Trust and Corporation Problems*, pp. 238ff.; p. 321.

GENERAL BIBLIOGRAPHY

Alderson, Bernard: *Andrew Carnegie: The Man and His Work;* New York, 1905.

American Antiquarian Society Proceedings, New Series. Vol. 29, "Greater New England in the Middle of the Nineteenth Century," by F. J. Turner.

American Bankers Association Bulletin, July, 1927, "Thrift—No Dilemma."

American Economic Association, *Economic Studies.* Vol. 1, Aug., 1896. Third Series. Vol. 1, 1900, "Influence of the Trust in the Development of Under-taking Genius," by S. Sherwood.

American Economic Association, *Proceedings,* Nov., 1907, "The Growth of Large Fortunes," by G. P. Watkins.

American Historical Review. Vol. 12, p. 761, "Rise of Manufacturing in the Miami Country," by F. P. Goodwin.

American Magazine, September and October, 1915, "Thrift," by A. S. Johnson.

Atlantic Monthly. Vol. 137, p. 533, 1926, "The Dilemma of Thrift."

Bacon, L. W., *A History of American Christianity,* New York, 1897.

Bankers Magazine. Vol. 77, p. 871; Vol. 86, pp. 117, 180, 570, 572; Vol. 92, p. 24; Vol. 93, p. 50; Vol. 94, p. 73; Vol. 97, p. 38.

Barrows, W., *United States of Yesterday and Tomorrow,* Boston, 1888.

Bayne, Samuel Gamble, *The Autobiography of Samuel Gamble Bayne, Derricks of Destiny,* New York, 1924.

Beard, Charles A. and Mary, *The Rise of American Civilization,* 2 Vols., New York, 1927.

Berglund, A., *The United States Steel Corporation, Columbia Studies in History, Economics, and Public Law.* Vol. 27, No. 2, 1907.

Birkbeck, Morris, *Notes on a Journey in America from the Coast of Virginia to the Territory of Illinois,* London and Dublin, 1818.

Bogart, E. L., and Thompson, C. M., *Readings in Economic History,* New York, 1916.

Boston Transcript, May 20 and 27, June 3, 10, 17, 24, July 1, 1905. Stories of land grabbing in the West.

Bridge, J. H., *The Inside History of the Carnegie Steel Company,* New York, 1903.

Brown, G. W., *Old Times in Oildom,* 1909.

Brunson, Alfred, *Western Pioneers,* Cincinnati, 1872.

Buck, S. J., *Illinois in 1818, Centennial History of Illinois.* Vol. 1, Springfield, 1917.
    The Granger Movement, a Study of Agricultural Organization and its Political, Economic, and Social Manifestations, 1870-1880, Cambridge, 1913.

Carnegie, Andrew, *Autobiography of Andrew Carnegie,* Boston, 1920.
    The Empire of Business, New York, 1902.
    The Gospel of Wealth and Other Timely Essays, New York, 1901.
    Triumphant Democracy, New York, 1886.

Carver, T. N., *The Present Economic Revolution in the United States,* New York, 1922.

Casson, H. N., *The Romance of Steel,* New York, 1907.

Century Magazine. Vol. 60, May, 1900, "Popular Illusions about Trusts," by Andrew Carnegie.

Cole, A. C., *The Era of the Civil War, 1848-1870, Centennial History of Illinois.* Vol. 3, Springfield, 1919.

Coman, Katharine, *Industrial History of the United States*, New York, 1911.

Chase, Stuart, and Schlink, F. J., *Your Money's Worth*, New York, 1927.

Chicago Historical Society MSS. Vol. 52.

Christian Examiner, Boston, 1824-1869.

Clews, Henry, *Men and Mysteries of Wall Street*.

Commons, John R., ed. *Documentary History of American Industrial Society*, 10 vols., Cleveland, 1909-1911. Vols. 1 and 2, on "Plantation and Frontier," by U. B. Phillips.

Commercial and Financial Chronicle.

Cosmopolitan, 1902, p. 292, article by D. O. Mills; Vol. 45, 1908, article by Charles M. Schwab, and article on "Owners of America."

Cubberly, E. P., *Public Education in the United States*, Boston, 1919.

Current Opinion. Vol. 54, "Extravagance as a Virtue," by S. N. Patten.

Davis, E., *The Half Century*, 1851.

Dictionary of American Biography.

Doddridge, Joseph, *Notes on the Settlement and Indian Wars of the Western Parts of Virginia and Pennsylvania from 1763 to 1783, inclusive, together with a review of the state of society and manners of the first settlement of the western country.* Dated June 17, 1824, Wellsburg, Virginia. First Edition.

Douglas, P. H., *Wages and the Family*, Chicago, 1925.

Drake, Daniel, *Pioneer Life in Kentucky, Reminiscential Letters from Daniel Drake, M.D., to his Children, 1870, Ohio Valley Historical Series*, No. 6, Cincinnati.

Epstein, A., *The Challenge of the Aged*, New York, 1928.

Essays in American History Dedicated to F. J. Turner, New York, 1910.

Ellsworth, H. L., *Illinois in 1837; a sketch descriptive of the situation, boundaries, face of the country . . . agricultural productions, public lands, plans of internal improvement, manufactures, etc., of the State of Illinois*, Philadelphia, 1837.

Fergus Historical Series. Vol. 1, No. 13, 1880. "Recollections of Early Illinois and her Noted Men," by J. Gillespie. Vol. 1, No. 14, 1881, "Early Society in Southern Illinois," by R. W. Patterson.

Fish, C. R., *The Rise of the Common Man, 1830-1850*, New York, 1927.

Flagg, Edmund, *The Far West, or, A Tour Beyond the Mountains*, 2 Vols. New York, 1838.

Flagler, H. M. (1830-1913), *In Memoriam*, New York Public Library.

Flint, Timothy, *History and Geography of the Mississippi Valley*, second edition, Cincinnati, 1832.
Recollections of the Last Ten Years, Boston, 1826.

Ford, Henry, and Crowthers, Samuel, *Today and Tomorrow*, New York, 1926.

Ford, Thomas, *History of Illinois, 1818-1847*, Chicago, 1854.

Franklin, Benjamin, *The Writings of Benjamin Franklin*, 10 Vols., New York, 1905-1907. A. H. Smyth, ed.

Gephart, W. F., *Transportation and Industrial Development in the Middle West, Columbia University Studies in History, Economics, and Public Law.* Vol. 34, No. 1, 1909.

Goodrich, G. G., *Recollections of a Lifetime.* Vol. 1, New York, 1857.

Grund, F. J., *The Americans*, 2 Vols., London, 1837.

Hall, Francis, *Travels in Canada and the United States in 1816 and 1817*, Boston, 1818.

Hall, James, *The Romance of Western History, or Sketches of History, Life, and Manners, in the West.* 2 Vols., Cincinnati, 1857.
Letters from the West, London, 1828.

Hamilton, T., *Men and Manners in America*, Ed.ʒburgh, 1834.

Haney, L. H., *Business Organization and Combination*, revised edition, New York, 1914.

Harvey, George B., *Henry Clay Frick, The Man*, New York and London, 1928.

Hazard, L. L., *The Frontier in American Literature*, New York, 1927.

Hendrick, B. J., *The Age of Big Business*, New Haven, 1919.

Hildreth, S. P., *Original Contributions to the "American Pioneer."* Cincinnati, 1844.

Hill, Robert T., *The Public Domain and Democracy*, New York, 1910.

Holliday, F. C., *Indiana Methodism: being an account of Methodism in the State*, Cincinnati, 1873.

Houghton, W. R., *Kings of Fortune or the Triumphs and Achievements of Noble, Self-Made Men*, New York, 1885.

Howe, D. W., *The Puritan Republic of the Massachusetts Bay*, Indianapolis, 1899.

Howe, Frederick C., *Privilege and Democracy in America*, New York, 1910.

Howells, W. C., *Recollections of Life in Ohio, 1813-40*, with an introduction by his son, W. D. Howells, Cincinnati, 1895.

Illinois State Historical Society Journal. Vol. 19, 1926, "The Daniel Boone Myth," by C. W. Alvord.

Illinois State Historical Society Transactions, 1905, "Puritan Influences," by Kofoid.

Indiana Magazine of History. Vol. 3, March, 1907, "Pioneer Life," by Parker. Also Vol. 10.

Independent Magazine, May 1, 1902, "The Concentration of Wealth," a symposium. October 8, 29, Nov. 5, 1908, on J. D. Archbold's relation to politics. June, 30, 1910, "The Thriftless Generation," and "The Discouragement of Thrift."

Iron Age, Oct., 1898, for a sketch of Gary.

Jones, A. D., *Illinois and the West*, Boston, 1838.

Journal of the American Statistical Association, Dec., 1922, p. 458, article by W. I. King.

Journal of the National Education Association. Vol. 95, p. 49, "Thrift—a Patriotic Necessity."

Journal of Political Economy. Vol. 18, 1910, "Pioneer Industry in the West," by Lippincott. Vol. 24, 1918, "Economics and Modern Psychology," by J. M. Clark.

King, Rufus, *Ohio, First Fruits of the Ordinance of 1787*, Boston, 1888.

Leaton, J., *History of Methodism in Illinois from 1793 to 1832*, Cincinnati, 1883.

Lewis, George, *Impressions of America and the American Churches*, Edinburgh, 1845.

Literary Digest. Nov., 1913, "The Unthrifty American." Dec. 29, 1928, concerning Henry Ford. Vol. 91, No. 86, "Is a Thrift Wave on the Way?"

Living Age, Feb. 17, 1912, "Thrift."

Lloyd, H. D., *Wealth Against Commonwealth*, New York, 1898.

Lyell, Sir Charles, *Travels in North America, 1841-1842*, 2 Vols., London, 1845.

McClure's Magazine, Nov., 1901, on the lives of important people in the U. S. Steel. Vol. 25, "The Character of John D. Rockefeller," by Ida Tarbell.

McGuffie, *Fifth Reader*, Cincinnati and New York, 1879.

Macleod, W. H., *The American Indian Frontier*, New York, 1928.

Mathews, L. K., *The Expansion of New England*, Boston, 1909.

Martineau, Harriett, *Society in America, 1834-1836*, 3 Vols., London, 1838.

Mazur, Paul, *American Prosperity, its Causes and Consequences*, New York, 1928.

Mesick, Jane L., *The English Traveller in America 1785-1835*, New York, 1922.

Methodist Magazine and Review. Vol. 19, 1837, "Happiness in a Cottage."

Methodist Quarterly Review. Vol. 39, 1857, "Influences of Methodism upon the Civilization and Education of the West," by T. M. Eddy. Vol. 53, 1871, "Early Methodism in the West."

Methodist Review. Vol. 54, 1872, "Peter Cartwright and Preaching in the West." Vol. 55, 1873.

Michigan Pioneer and Historical Collections. Vol. 38, "Personal Recollections of Pioneer Days," by Ruth Hoppin.

Minnesota Historical Collection. Vol. 8, "Advent of Commerce in Minnesota."

Minnesota History, June and September, 1928, article on "Land Claim Association."

Mississippi Historical Society Publication. Vol. 4, 1901, "Recollections of Pioneer Life in Mississippi," by M. J. Welsh.

Mississippi Valley Historical Association Proceedings. Vols. 3, 5, 9, 15.

Missouri Historical Review, Vol. 3, "German Communistic Society in Missouri," by Beck.

Montague, G. H., *The Rise and Progress of the Standard Oil Company*, New York, 1903.

Moody, John, *The Masters of Capital*, New Haven, 1919.

Moulton, H. G., *The Financial Organization of Society*, Chicago, 1925.

Mussey, H. R., *Combination in the Mining Industry: A Study of Concentration in Lake Superior Iron Ore Production, Columbia University Studies in History, Economics, and Public Law.* Vol. 23, No. 3, New York, 1905.

Nation, Feb. 16, 1921, "The Menace of Thrift."

National Bureau of Economic Research, *Income in the United States*, New York, 1921, and, *Recent Economic Changes.* 2 Vols., New York, 1929.

National Education Association, *Reports*, 1918, 1924, 1925.

National Industrial Conference Board, *Employee Stock Purchase Plans in the United States*, and *Employee Thrift and Investment Plans*, New York, 1929.

Nearing, Scott, *Social Adjustment*, 1908, New York.

Nevins, A., *Emergence of Modern America, 1865-1878*, New York 1927.

New Republic. Vol. 29, 1921-1922, Vol. 33, 1922-1923, Vol. 37, 1923-1924, Vol. 42, 1925, "Thrift," by David Friday.

Niebuhr, H. Richard, *The Social Sources of Denominationalism*, New York, 1929.

Nineteenth Century and After, February and April, 1916.

North American Review, September, 1909, "The Agrarian Revolution in the Middle West," by J. B. Ross.

Noyes, A. D., *Forty Years of American Finance*, New York, 1909.

Ohio Archæological and Historical Society Publications. Vol. 14, 1905, "Early Cincinnati," by J. Wilby.

Parrington, V. L., *Main Currents in American Thought, An Interpretation of American Literature from the Beginnings to 1920.* 2 Vols., New York, 1927. Vol. 1, 1620-1800. *The Colonial Mind.* Vol. 2, 1800-1860. *The Romantic Revolution in America.*

Pease, T. C., *The Frontier State, 1818-1848, Centennial History of Illinois.* Vol. 2, Springfield, 1918.

Peck, J. M., *A New Guide for Emigrants to the West*, 2nd edition, Boston, 1837. *Forty Years of Pioneer Life, Memoirs of J. M. Peck, edited from his journals and correspondence, by Rufus Babcock*, Philadelphia, 1864.

Political Science Quarterly. Vol. 22, 1907, article on "Thrift", and Vol. 224, 1914.

Pooley, W. V., *The Settlement of Illinois from 1830-1850, University of Wisconsin History Series Bulletin.* Vol. 1, No. 220.

Pound, Roscoe, *Spirit of the Common Law. ch.* on "Frontier and the Law: Puritanism and the Law."

Powell, L. W., ed. *Historic Towns of the Western States*, New York and London, 1900.

Presbyterian Historical Society Journal. Vol. 12, "Influence of Presbyterian Church in Early American History," by H. D. Funk.

Princeton University Industrial Section, *Employee Savings Plans*, Princeton, 1929.

Quaife, M. M., *Chicago and the Old Northwest*, 1673-1835, Chicago, 1913.

Reed, H. B., *The Morals of Monopoly and Competition*, Menasha, Wisconsin, 1916.

Reynolds, J., *My Own Times, Embracing also the History of My Life*, Belleville, Ill., 1855.

Ripley, W. Z., ed. *Trusts, Pools and Corporations*, revised edition, Boston and New York, 1916.

Ripley, W. Z., Main Street and Wall Street, Boston, 1927.

Rockefeller, John D., *Random Reminiscences of Men and Events*, New York, 1909.

Roosevelt, T., *The Winning of the West*, 4 Vols., New York, 1889, 1896.

Ryan, J. A., *A Living Wage*, New York, 1912.

Rusk, Ralph L., *The Literature of the Middle Western Frontier.* 2 Vols., New York, 1925.

Russell, Phillips, *Benjamin Franklin, The First Civilized American*, New York, 1926.

Schoolcraft, H. R., *Travels in the Central Portions of the Mississippi Valley*, New York, 1825.

Schultz, Christian, Jr., *Travels on an Inland Voyage Through the States of New York, Pennsylvania, Virginia, Ohio, Kentucky, and Tennessee, and Through the Territories of Indiana, Louisiana, Mississippi, and New Orleans in the Years 1807 and 1808.* 2 Vols., New York, 1810.

Seligman, E. R. A., *The Economics of Installment Selling.* 2 Vols., New York and London, 1927.

Shortridge, Wilson P., *Transition of a Typical Frontier*, Menasha, Wisconsin, 1922.

Sombart, Werner, *The Quintessence of Capitalism*, New York, 1915.

South Atlantic Quarterly. Vol. 4, 1906, "Our Legacy from a Century of Pioneers," by Albert Shaw.

Stevens, Walter B., *Missourians One Hundred Years Ago*, Columbia, Mo., 1917.

Straus, S. W., *History of the Thrift Movement in America*, New York, 1920.

Streightoff, F. H., *The Standard of Living*, New York, 1911.

Sullivan, Mark, *Our Times.* 2 Vols., New York and London, 1927.

Sun (New York), May 20, 1909, re H. H. Rogers.

Sweet, W. W., *The Rise of Methodism in the West; being the Journal of the Western Conference, 1800-1811, ed. with notes and introduction*, New York and Cincinnati, 1920.

Tarbell, Ida M., *History of the Standard Oil Company.* 2 Vols., New York, 1904. *The Life of Elbert H. Gary*, New York, 1925.

Tawney, R. H., *Religion and the Rise of Capitalism*, New York and London, 1926.

Thwaites, Reuben G., *Early Western Travels, 1748-1846; a series of annotated reprints of some of the best and rarest contemporary volumes of travel, descriptive of the aborigines and social and economic conditions in the middle and far west.* Vols., 3, 9, 10, 19, Cleveland, 1904-1907.

Times (New York), May 20, 1909, re H. H. Rogers.

de Tocqueville, A., *Democracy in America*, American edition. 2 Vols., Boston, 1873.

Tribune (New York), May 20, 1909, re H. H. Rogers.

Tryon, Rolla M., *Household Manufactures in the United States, 1640-1860, A Study in Industrial History*, Chicago, 1917.

Turner, F. J., *The Frontier in American History*, New York, 1920.
The Rise of the New West, New York, 1906.

U. S. Bureau of Corporations, *Report of the Commissioner of Corporations on the Petroleum Industry*, 2 Vols., Washington, 1907.
Report of the Commissioner of Corporations on the Steel Industry, 2 Parts, Washington, 1911-1912.

U. S. Industrial Commission, *Report*. Vols., I, II, XIII, Washington, 1901.

Veblen, Thorstein, *Absentee Ownership*, New York, 1923.

Vogel, Rachel, *Social Life in St. Louis (1764-1804)*. Unpublished manuscript in New York Public Library.

Volwiler, A. T., *Croghan and the Westward Movement*, New York, 1926.

Ware, N. J., *The Industrial Worker, 1840-1860*, Boston, 1924.

Watkins, M. W., *Industrial Combinations and Public Policy*, New York, 1927.

Weber, Max, *Gesammelte Aufsatze Zur Religionssoziologie*, Vol. I, Tubingen, 1920.

Western Reserve Historical Society Tracts. Vol. 4, "Farm Life in Central Ohio," by Welker.

Weyland, J. W., *German Element in the Shenandoah Valley of Virginia*, 1907.

Wilgus, H. L., *A Study of the U. S. Steel Corporation in its Industrial and Legal Aspects*, Chicago, 1901.

Williams, J. M., *The Expansion of Rural Life*, New York, 1926.

Williams, Sherman, *Some Successful Americans*, Boston, 1904.

Wisconsin Historical Collections. Vol. 15, "Methodist Circuit Rider's Tour from Pennsylvania to Wisconsin, 1835."

Wisconsin Magazine of History. Vol. 7.

Worth, G. A., *Random Recollections of Albany, 1800-1808*, which includes *Recollections of Cincinnati, 1817-1821*, published in 1850.

Youngman, Anna, *The Economic Causes of Great Fortunes*, New York, 1907.

INDEX

DONALD W. McCONNELL

Born in Ipswich, Massachusetts, October 8, 1901.
A.B., Ohio Wesleyan University, 1923.
A.M., Columbia University, 1927.
Instructor in Economics in the Washington Square College
of New York University, 1928- ———.

Big Business

Economic Power in a Free Society

An Arno Press Collection

Alsberg, Carl L. **Combination in the American Bread-Baking Industry:** With Some Observations on the Mergers of 1924-25. 1926

Armes, Ethel. **The Story of Coal and Iron in Alabama.** 1910

Atkinson, Edward. **The Industrial Progress of the Nation:** Consumption Limited, Production Unlimited. 1889

Baker, John Calhoun. **Directors and Their Functions:** A Preliminary Study. 1945

Barron, Clarence W. **More They Told Barron:** Conversations and Revelations of an American Pepys in Wall Street. 1931

Bossard, James H. S. and J. Frederic Dewhurst. **University Education For Business:** A Study of Existing Needs and Practices. 1931

Bridge, James H., editor. **The Trust:** Its Book. Being a Presentation of the Several Aspects of the Latest Form of Industrial Evolution. 1902

Civic Federation of Chicago. **Chicago Conference on Trusts.** 1900

Clews, Henry. **Fifty Years in Wall Street.** 1908

Coman, Katharine. **The Industrial History of the United States.** 1910

Crafts, Wilbur F. **Successful Men of To-Day:** And What They Say of Success. 1883

Davis, John P. **The Union Pacific Railway:** A Study in Railway Politics, History, and Economics. 1894

Economics and Social Justice. 1973

Edie, Lionel D., editor. **The Stabilization of Business.** 1923

Edwards, Richard, editor. **New York's Great Industries.** 1884

Ely, Richard T. **Monopolies and Trusts.** 1912

Ford, Henry. **My Life and Work.** 1922

Freedley, Edwin T. **A Practical Treatise on Business.** 1853

Hadley, Arthur Twining. **Standards of Public Morality.** 1907

Hamilton, Walton, et al. **Price and Price Policies.** 1938

Haney, Lewis H. **Business Organization and Combination.** 1914

Hill, James J. **Highways of Progress.** 1910

Jenks, Jeremiah Whipple and Walter E. Clark. **The Trust Problem.** Fifth Edition. 1929

Keezer, Dexter Merriam and Stacy May. **The Public Control of Business.** 1930

La Follette, Robert Marion, editor. **The Making of America:** Industry and Finance. 1905

Lilienthal, David E. **Big Business:** A New Era. 1952

Lippincott, Isaac. **A History of Manufactures in the Ohio Valley to the Year 1860.** 1914

Lloyd, Henry Demarest. **Lords of Industry.** 1910

McConnell, Donald. **Economic Virtues in the United States.** 1930

Mellon, Andrew W. **Taxation:** The People's Business. 1924

Meyer, Balthasar Henry. **Railway Legislation in the United States.** 1909

Mills, James D. **The Art of Money Making.** 1872

Montague, Gilbert Holland. **The Rise and Progress of the Standard Oil Company.** 1904

Mosely Industrial Commission. **Reports of the Delegates of the Mosely Industrial Commission to the United States of America, Oct.-Dec., 1902.** 1903

Orth, Samuel P., compiler. **Readings on the Relation of Government to Property and Industry.** 1915

Patten, Simon N[elson]. **The Economic Basis of Protection.** 1890

Peto, Sir S[amuel] Morton. **Resources and Prospects of America.** 1866

Ripley, William Z[ebina]. **Main Street and Wall Street.** 1929

Ripley, William Z[ebina]. **Railroads:** Rates and Regulation. 1912

Rockefeller, John D. **Random Reminiscences of Men and Events.** 1909

Seager, Henry R. and Charles A. Gulick, Jr. **Trust and Corporation Problems.** 1929

Taeusch, Carl F. **Policy and Ethics in Business.** 1931

Taylor, Albion Guilford. **Labor Policies of the National Association of Manufacturers.** 1928

Vanderlip, Frank A. **Business and Education.** 1907

Van Hise, Charles R. **Concentration and Control:** A Solution of the Trust Problem in the United States. 1912

The Wealthy Citizens of New York. 1973

White, Bouck. **The Book of Daniel Drew.** 1910

Wile, Frederic William, editor. **A Century of Industrial Progress.** 1928

Wilgus, Horace L. **A Study of the United States Steel Corporation in Its Industrial and Legal Aspects.** 1901

[Youmans, Edward L., compiler] **Herbert Spencer on the Americans.** 1883

Youngman, Anna. **The Economic Causes of Great Fortunes.** 1909